# Understanding the Weather

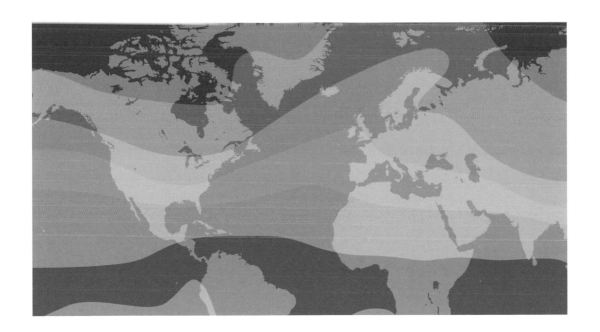

WORLD ALMANAC® LIBRARY

Please visit our web site at: www.worldalmanaclibrary.com
For a free color catalog describing World Almanac® Library's
list of high-quality books and multimedia programs,
call 1-800-848-2928 or fax your request to (414) 332-3567.

The editors at World Almanac® Library would like to thank Dr. Jonathan D. Kahl, Professor of Atmospheric
Science, University of Wisconsin-Milwaukee for the technical expertise and advice he brought to the
production of this book.

Library of Congress Cataloging-in-Publication Data available upon request from publisher.
Fax (414) 336-0157 for the attention of the Publishing Records Department.

ISBN 0-8368-5009-2

This North American edition first published in 2002 by
**World Almanac® Library**
330 West Olive Street, Suite 100
Milwaukee, WI 53212  USA

Created and produced as the *Visual Guide to Understanding Climate and the Environment* by
QA INTERNATIONAL
329 rue de la Commune Ouest, 3ᵉ étage
Montreal, Québec
Canada H2Y 2E1
Tel: (514) 499-3000  Fax: (514) 499-3010
www.qa-international.com

© QA International, 2001

**Publisher:** Jacques Fortin

**Editorial Director:** François Fortin

**Executive Editor:** Serge D'Amico

**Illustrations Editor:** Marc Lalumière

**Art Director:** Rielle Lévesque

**Graphic Designer:** Anne Tremblay

**Writers:** Stéphane Batigne, Josée Bourbonnière, Nathalie Fredette, Agence Science-Presse

**Computer Graphic Artists:** Jean-Yves Ahern, Maxime Bigras, Patrice Blais, Yan Bohler, Mélanie Boivin,
Charles Campeau, Jocelyn Gardner, Jonathan Jacques, Alain Lemire, Raymond Martin, Nicolas Oroc,
Carl Pelletier, Simon Pelletier, Frédérick Simard, Mamadou Togola, Yan Tremblay

**Researchers:** Anne-Marie Brault, Jessie Daigle, Anne-Marie Villeneuve, Kathleen Wynd

**Translation:** Käthe Roth

**Copy Editor:** Jane Broderick

**Production:** Mac Thien Nguyen Hoang

**Prepress:** Tony O'Riley

**Page Layout:** Véronique Boisvert, Lucie Mc Brearty, Geneviève Théroux Béliveau

**Reviewers:** Gilles Brien, Yves Comeau, Frédéric Fabry, David B. Frost, Mario Laquerre, Marc Olivier,
Judith Patterson

**World Almanac® Library Editor:** Alan Wachtel

**World Almanac® Library Art Direction:** Tammy Gruenewald

**Cover Design:** Katherine A. Goedheer

**Photo credits:** abbreviations: t = top, c = center, b = bottom, r = right, l = left
p. 13 (br) (Winds): Sharron Sample, Chief Information Officer, Earth Science Enterprise, NASA. Courtesy of
NASA; p. 15 (tl) (Jet stream): Calvin J. Hamilton, Views of the Solar System. Courtesy of NASA; p. 20 (cr)
(Tornado): AFP/CORBIS/Magma; p. 25 (br, bc) (Water vapor, Clouds): Zoë Hall, Eumetsat User Service,
© Eumetsat 2001; p. 41 (br) (Hurricane): Bert Ulrich, Public Services Division, NASA Headquarters. Courtesy
of NASA; p. 53 (c) (Radar image): Frédéric Fabry, Radar Observatory of McGill University, Montreal; p. 54 (c)
(visible, infrared, water vapor): Zoë Hall, Eumetsat User Service, © Eumetsat 2001; p. 54 (bl) (Composite
image): Zoë Hall, Eumetsat User Service, © Eumetsat 2001; p. 56 (cl) (Mediterranean storm): Image and
data processing by National Geophysical Data Center of NOAA; p. 56 (br) (Ocean temperatures): Courtesy of
NOAA; p. 57 (tl) (Mount Vesuvius): Courtesy of NASA/GSFC/MITI/ERSDAC/JAROS, and U.S./Japan ASTER
Science Team; p. 59 (bl) (Turbulence): Pierre Tourigny, Meteorological Service of Canada. Image reproduced
with the permission of the Minister of Public Works and Government Services of Canada, 2001.

Printed in Canada

1 2 3 4 5 6 7 8 9 06 05 04 03 02

# Table of
# Contents

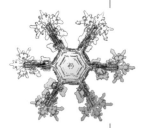

The air that we breathe is part of the atmosphere, the thin gaseous layer that surrounds Earth and protects it from the dangerous types of solar radiation. Like all other matter, air has weight, but this weight varies greatly depending on altitude and temperature. Variations in pressure cause atmospheric movements in which large air masses collide with or slide by each other. Winds, light or strong, constant or unpredictable, contribute to the planet's thermal equilibrium.

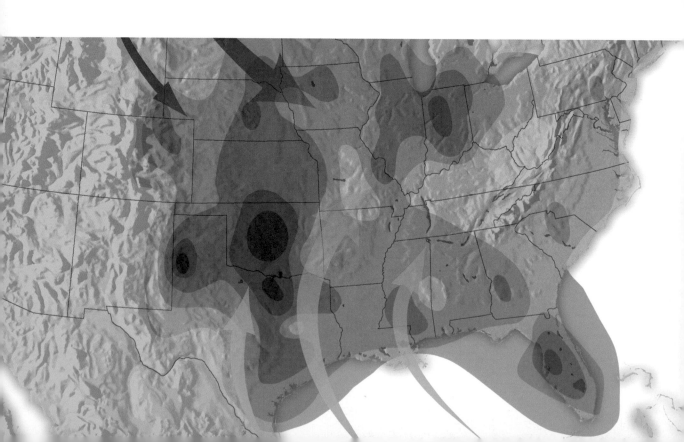

# Earth's Atmosphere

# The Atmosphere

## *A thin, protective layer*

The atmosphere, defined as the gaseous envelope surrounding Earth, does not have a well-defined upper edge. Half of its air molecules are concentrated in the 3-mile (5-kilometer) -thick layer just above Earth, but there are still traces of air at more than 620 miles (1,000 km) altitude. Because of their protective function, the layers of the atmosphere are essential to the existence of life on Earth. All of the major meteorological phenomena also occur in the atmosphere.

### THE COMPOSITION OF AIR

Below 50 miles (80 km), the composition of the atmosphere remains stable. Nitrogen and oxygen make up about 99 percent of its volume. Other gases, including argon and neon, are also found in air, but in much smaller quantities. The proportions of water vapor and carbon dioxide in the atmosphere vary but are always small.

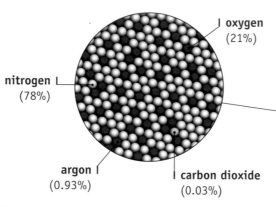

**oxygen**
(21%)

**nitrogen**
(78%)

**argon**
(0.93%)

**carbon dioxide**
(0.03%)

**radiosonde**
22 miles
(35 km)

### SOLAR ENERGY

In the Sun's core, nuclear fusion reactions maintain a temperature of 15 million degrees. This huge amount of energy, constantly radiating into space in the form of electromagnetic rays, heats Earth's surface and enables life to exist and develop on the planet.

**Solar radiation,** or energy from the Sun, covers the entire electromagnetic spectrum.

**supersonic jet**
59,060 feet
(18,000 meters)

**airliner**
36,090 feet
(11,000 m)

**Mount Everest**
29,028 feet
(8,848 m)

The **atmosphere** and clouds reflect 30 percent of solar radiation.

The **mesosphere**, at 31–50 miles (50–80 km) high, is the coldest layer of the atmosphere. At its outside edge, the temperature is as low as –148° Fahrenheit (–100° Celsius).

30 miles
(50 km)

## THE LAYERS OF THE ATMOSPHERE

Earth's atmosphere is made up of layers. Starting at Earth's surface, the temperature typically decreases at higher altitudes through the troposphere. In the next layer, the stratosphere, temperatures begin to increase. Above the stratosphere is the mesosphere, in which temperatures again decrease with increasing altitude. In the thermosphere (50–310 miles [80–500 km] altitude), the layer above the mesosphere, temperatures rise greatly, since this layer absorbs a great deal of solar radiation. Above the thermosphere is the exosphere, the zone where the few remaining molecules of air escape Earth's gravity.

The temperature at the bottom of the **stratosphere** (9–31 miles [15–50 km]) rises from –71°F (–57°C) to 32°F (0°C) at the top because of absorption of solar radiation by stratospheric ozone.

The **ozone layer**, located mainly between 13 and 19 miles (20 and 30 km) altitude, intercepts much of the Sun's ultraviolet radiation directed toward Earth.

The **tropopause** is the border between the troposphere and the stratosphere. Its altitude varies depending on the season, the temperature on Earth's surface, the latitude, and the atmospheric pressure.

9 miles
(15 km)    The tops of **cumulonimbus** clouds can reach, and even go beyond, the edge of the troposphere.

The **sky** is blue because air molecules scatter mainly short-wave radiation, which corresponds to the color blue in the visible spectrum.

Most meteorological phenomena occur in the **troposphere** (0–9 miles [0–15 km]), the layer that contains almost all the atmosphere's water vapor.

At **sea level**, the average temperature of the atmosphere is 59°F (15°C).

# Atmospheric Pressure

## The weight of air

Because molecules obey the laws of gravity, the molecules in the gases that make up Earth's atmosphere have a certain weight, which we bear constantly without being aware of it. Atmospheric pressure is the force that air exerts by weighing on a given area. At sea level, this pressure is equivalent to an average of 1,013 hectopascals (hPa), or 14 pounds per square inch (1.013 kilograms per square centimeter).

Various factors, such as altitude and temperature, can create zones of high and low atmospheric pressure. These variations are directly linked to major meteorological phenomena.

### HOW AIR PRESSURE IS MEASURED

The mercury barometer is used to measure atmospheric pressure. Air presses on the mercury contained in a reservoir, forcing it to rise in an evacuated tube. The pressure exerted by the air is measured according to the level reached by the mercury. For a long time, the height of the mercury was the unit of measurement of atmospheric pressure. Today, the International System uses the hectopascal (hPa); 1,000 hPa is equivalent to the pressure exerted by a 2.2-pound (1-kg) mass on an area measuring .15 in$^2$ (1 cm$^2$).

vacuum

At sea level, the height of the mercury is, on average, **30 inches** (76 cm).

tube

air pressure

mercury reservoir

### THE INFLUENCE OF ALTITUDE ON ATMOSPHERIC PRESSURE

The higher we go, the less air there is above us. Atmospheric pressure therefore drops with altitude. In the lower troposphere, this drop in pressure is quite constant, falling about 1 hPa every 29 feet (8.5 meters).

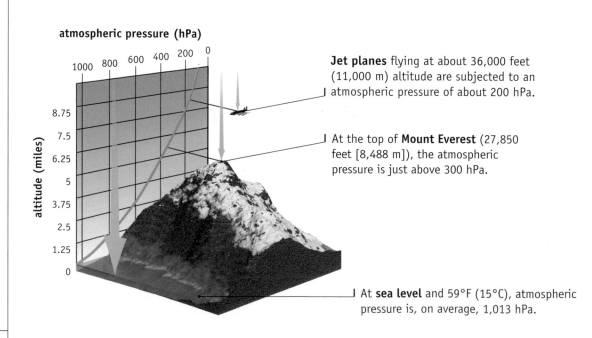

atmospheric pressure (hPa)

1000   800   600   400   200   0

altitude (miles)

8.75
7.5
6.25
5
3.75
2.5
1.25
0

**Jet planes** flying at about 36,000 feet (11,000 m) altitude are subjected to an atmospheric pressure of about 200 hPa.

At the top of **Mount Everest** (27,850 feet [8,488 m]), the atmospheric pressure is just above 300 hPa.

At **sea level** and 59°F (15°C), atmospheric pressure is, on average, 1,013 hPa.

## HOW TEMPERATURE AFFECTS ATMOSPHERIC PRESSURE

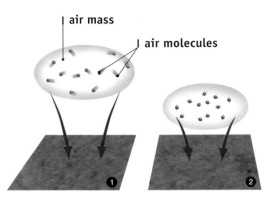

air mass

air molecules

When an air mass cools ❶, the molecules in it slow down. This slowing makes the air mass contract and become denser and thus heavier. It descends toward the ground ❷, where it creates a high-pressure zone, or anticyclone ❸.

high-pressure zone

The heating of surface air ❹ causes the opposite effect. Molecules become more agitated and move farther away from each other, making the air mass less dense. As it becomes lighter than the surrounding air, the warm air mass rises ❺, leaving a low-pressure zone, or cyclone, at ground level ❻.

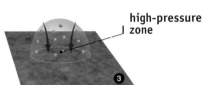

low-pressure zone

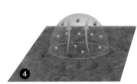

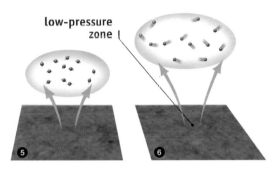

## THE DISTRIBUTION OF ANTICYCLONES AND CYCLONES AROUND THE PLANET

In general, anticyclones (high-pressure zones) and cyclones (low-pressure zones) alternate around Earth in wide, relatively parallel bands. Their patterns, however, are affected by the presence of the continents, whose land accentuates the warming or cooling of the air masses above them.

| ATMOSPHERIC PRESSURE (hPa) | |
| --- | --- |
| > 1032 | 1008–1014 |
| 1026–1032 | 1002–1008 |
| 1020–1026 | 996–1002 |
| 1014–1020 | < 996 |

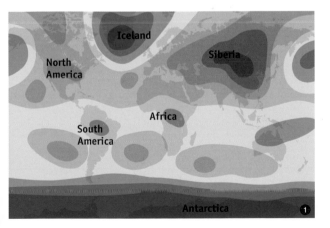

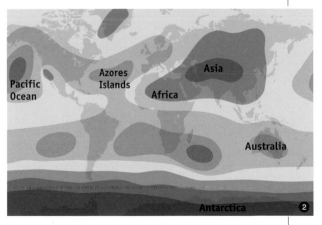

In **January** ❶, strong anticyclones settle over the continents in the Northern Hemisphere, sitting alongside the cyclones over the northern oceans. In equatorial regions, warm air rises and creates a belt of cyclones, particularly marked over the continents. In the Southern Hemisphere, where there is less land, tropical anticyclones are confined to the oceans, while cyclones sit over the subpolar regions.

In **July** ❷, the heat that is prevalent in Asia maintains a huge low-pressure zone that extends as far as Africa. The oceans in the Northern Hemisphere are under high-pressure zones (the Azores and Pacific anticyclones), but the subpolar depressions have almost disappeared. In the Southern Hemisphere, a broad anticyclonic belt settles over all the tropical regions, both continental and oceanic. The low-pressure zone that sits above the Antarctic coast varies little.

# The Movement of Air Masses

*Fronts and cyclones*

An air mass is a large blob of air that acquires the temperature (warm or cold) and water vapor (humid or dry) characteristics of the underlying surface. As winds push the air masses, they come into contact with each other and thus help to distribute humidity and heat around the surface of the planet.

When two air masses with different temperatures and humidity levels meet, they do not mix, but collide along a line called a front. This encounter causes the formation of clouds and precipitation.

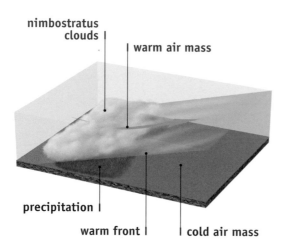

nimbostratus clouds

warm air mass

precipitation

warm front

cold air mass

## WARM FRONT

When a moving warm air mass overtakes a cold air mass, it creates a warm front. The warm air rises, since it is lighter, becoming cooler as it moves higher. The humidity that it contains condenses in the form of nimbostratus clouds. This configuration is often associated with moderate precipitation.

## COLD FRONT

A cold air mass that overtakes a warm air mass produces a cold front. The denser cold air slides under the warm air, which is forced to rise rapidly, forming cumulonimbus clouds. Then, heavy precipitation, sometimes with storms, develops.

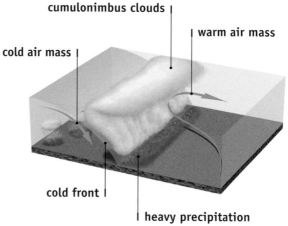

cumulonimbus clouds

warm air mass

cold air mass

cold front

heavy precipitation

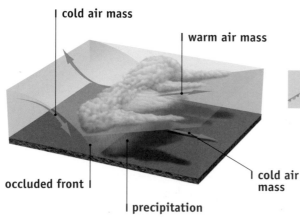

cold air mass

warm air mass

occluded front

precipitation

cold air mass

## OCCLUDED FRONT

An occlusion, or occluded front, occurs when a cold front overtakes a warm front. Two cold air masses join, surrounding the warm air mass and pushing it upward.

## AIR MASSES

Air masses are divided into six categories, according to the climatic characteristics (temperature and humidity) of the places where they are formed. As they are pushed by the winds, they directly influence the weather in the regions over which they move. Their characteristics slowly change, however, sometimes to the point where they become unrecognizable.

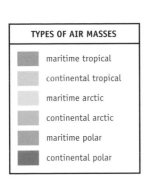

**TYPES OF AIR MASSES**

- maritime tropical
- continental tropical
- maritime arctic
- continental arctic
- maritime polar
- continental polar

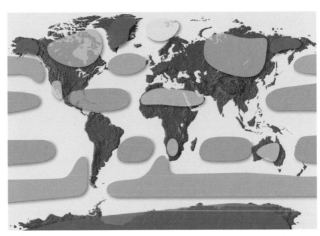

## HOW A CYCLONE FORMS AND DISSIPATES

When cold air masses from polar regions collide with warm air masses from the tropics, their meeting produces a front on which, at a particular point, the pressure begins to drop. Thus, a cyclone is born. Clouds, precipitation, and winds develop there until the cylcone dissipates.

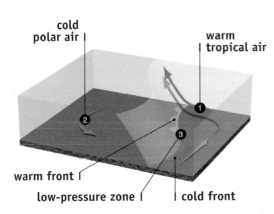

Lighter warm air ❶ rises above the cold air ❷, creating a low-pressure zone ❸ around which warm and cold fronts form.

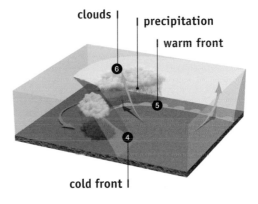

Sucked in by low pressure, the cold air begins to move in a circular pattern. The cold front ❹ approaches the warm front ❺. At a high altitude, the warm air condenses and forms clouds ❻, which drop precipitation.

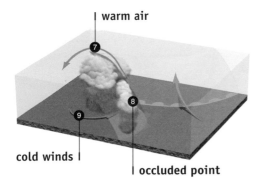

When the cold front overtakes the warm front, the warm air ❼ is pushed to a higher altitude, above the occlusion ❽. The weather is unstable and windy ❾.

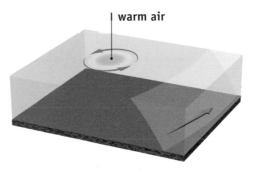

The occlusion finally blocks the inflow of warm air. As the cyclone then begins to dissipate, the wind subsides and precipitation stops.

# Winds

When air masses with different pressures are present in the atmosphere, the air is forced to move in currents called winds. Winds also carry the heat and humidity of the air masses and thus play an essential role in most meteorological phenomena.

## THE SPEED OF WINDS

Isobars, which are lines drawn on weather maps that link places with the same atmospheric pressure, reveal anticyclones and cyclones. Because they show the pressure gradient, defined as the difference in pressure between two zones as a function of their distance, isobars can also indicate wind speeds.

The center of a **cyclone**, or low-pressure zone, is shown by the letter L.

Isobars close together are the sign of a strong pressure gradient, which gives rise to **strong winds.**

A weak pressure gradient, indicated by isobars far from each other, is accompanied by **light winds.**

The letter H indicates the center of an **anticyclone** (high-pressure zone).

direction of Earth's rotation

isobar

1004 1000 996 **L** 1008 1012 1016 1020 1024 **H** 1016 1008 1012 1004 1012 1020 **H** 1016

North Pole

direction of Earth's rotation

theoretical path

real path

## THE CORIOLIS FORCE

Imagine a rocket traveling in a straight line from the North Pole to the equator, covering the distance in one hour. Since Earth rotates at a speed of 15° per hour, the target will have deviated from its position by 15° when the rocket lands. On Earth, the rocket appears to have deviated to the right. This deviation, called the Coriolis force, acts on all bodies in motion around Earth, including winds. In the Northern Hemisphere, it deflects all movement to the right, while, in the Southern Hemisphere, it shifts all movement to the left.

## WIND DIRECTIONS AT HIGH ALTITUDE AND AT GROUND LEVEL

The direction of a wind is the result of a combination of several forces. The pressure gradient ❶ pushes air in a straight line from a high-pressure zone to a low-pressure-zone. The Coriolis force ❷ deflects this movement to the right or the left, depending on the hemisphere. When nothing impedes these forces, as is the case at high altitude, the winds ❸ tend to blow parallel to the isobars. In the Northern Hemisphere, the winds turn clockwise around anticyclones and counterclockwise around cyclones.

But Earth itself exerts a friction force on the lowest portion of the atmosphere; air layers located below 1,640 feet (500 m) altitude are slowed down somewhat by the planet's motion, which diminishes the Coriolis force. Surface winds ❹ can therefore penetrate to the center of cyclones.

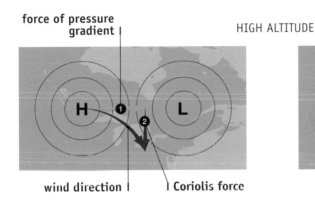

force of pressure gradient ❶

HIGH ALTITUDE

wind direction    Coriolis force

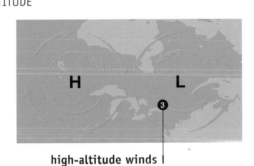

high-altitude winds

Coriolis force

SURFACE

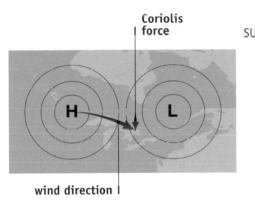

wind direction

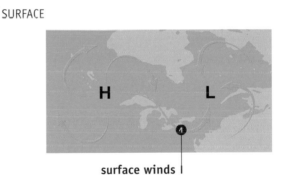

surface winds

## GENERAL ATMOSPHERIC CIRCULATION

From data obtained by weather satellites, computers produce maps simulating the general circulation of winds in Earth's atmosphere. The arrows indicate the direction of the winds, while the color zones indicate their speed. This image shows surface winds over the Pacific Ocean.

**APPROXIMATE WIND SPEEDS**

| (m/s) | (ft/s) |
|-------|--------|
| 0 | 0 |
| 2 | 6.5 |
| 4 | 13 |
| 6 | 19.5 |
| 8 | 26 |
| 10 | 32.5 |
| 12 | 39 |
| 14 | 45.5 |
| 16 | 52 |
| 18 | 58.5 |
| 20 | 65 |

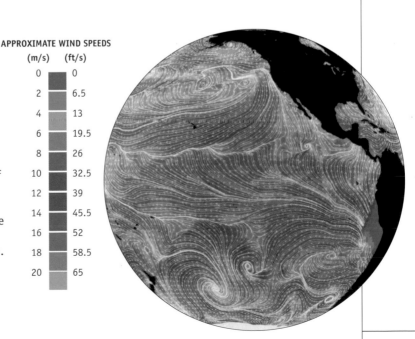

# Prevailing Winds

*Major atmospheric movements*

On the planetary scale, atmospheric circulation is organized in huge loops that combine vertical and horizontal movements of air masses. These remarkably constant circuits of air give rise to the prevailing surface winds, such as the trade winds. At high altitudes, the jet streams, which are also constant in direction, blow in circles around the globe at a very high speed.

### CELLS OF ATMOSPHERIC CIRCULATION

Above each of Earth's hemispheres are three loops of atmospheric circulation: the polar cell, the Ferrel cell, and the Hadley cell. These loops are composed of ascending and descending movements, caused by pressure gradients, and of horizontal movements, caused by the Coriolis force. In each circuit, the warm air rises, moves at high altitude, descends again as it cools, and then is warmed again as it moves on the surface in a constant direction.

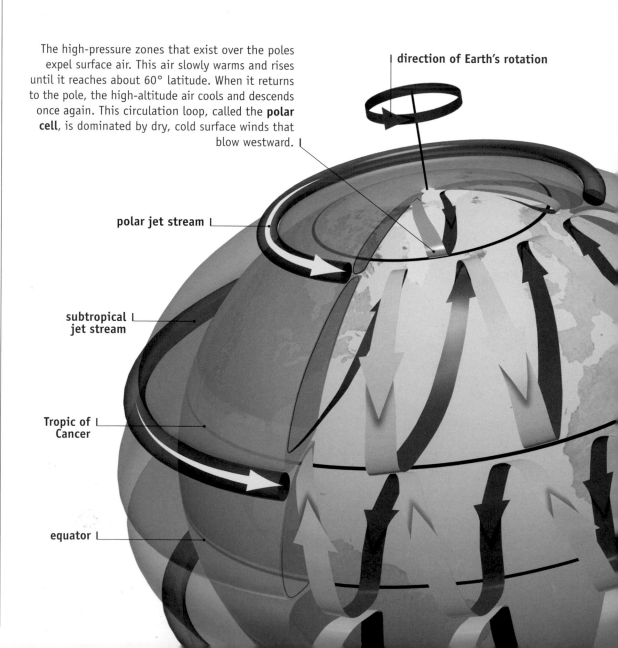

The high-pressure zones that exist over the poles expel surface air. This air slowly warms and rises until it reaches about 60° latitude. When it returns to the pole, the high-altitude air cools and descends once again. This circulation loop, called the **polar cell**, is dominated by dry, cold surface winds that blow westward.

direction of Earth's rotation

polar jet stream

subtropical jet stream

Tropic of Cancer

equator

## THE JET STREAMS

At very high altitudes of between 19,700 and 49,200 feet (6,000–15,000 m), very strong winds called the jet streams blow around Earth from west to east. They are divided into polar systems, located at about 60° latitude, and subtropical systems, found above the tropics.

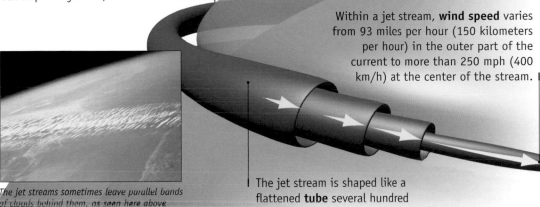

Within a jet stream, **wind speed** varies from 93 miles per hour (150 kilometers per hour) in the outer part of the current to more than 250 mph (400 km/h) at the center of the stream.

The jet streams sometimes leave parallel bands of clouds behind them, as seen here above Saudi Arabia.

The jet stream is shaped like a flattened **tube** several hundred miles (km) wide.

## ROSSBY WAVES

Jet streams do not always follow a straight path. When the polar jet stream is not moving fast enough, the Coriolis force causes it to undulate slightly ❶. This perturbation may be accentuated until large meanders, called Rossby waves, are formed ❷. The cyclones and anticyclones that develop within these loops ❸ have a major influence on the climate in the middle latitudes all around the planet.

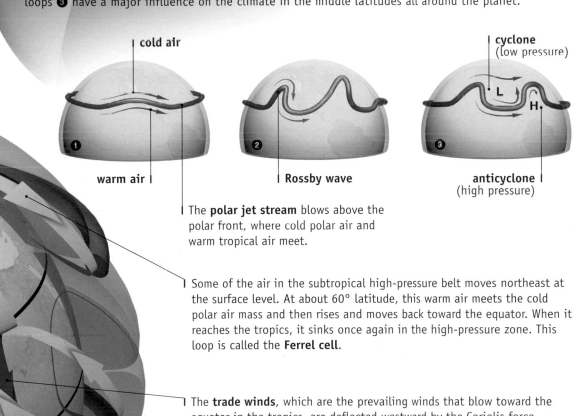

cold air

warm air

❶

Rossby wave

❷

cyclone
(low pressure)

L

H

anticyclone
(high pressure)

❸

The **polar jet stream** blows above the polar front, where cold polar air and warm tropical air meet.

Some of the air in the subtropical high-pressure belt moves northeast at the surface level. At about 60° latitude, this warm air meets the cold polar air mass and then rises and moves back toward the equator. When it reaches the tropics, it sinks once again in the high-pressure zone. This loop is called the **Ferrel cell**.

The **trade winds**, which are the prevailing winds that blow toward the equator in the tropics, are deflected westward by the Coriolis force.

Heated by the Sun, equatorial air rises to the tropopause, then moves toward the poles. As it changes altitude, the air cools, gets heavier, and returns toward the surface in the tropical latitudes. Expelled from this high-pressure zone, the dry air returns toward the equator, thus completing the atmospheric loop called the **Hadley cell**.

# Local Winds

## *The results of relief features*

Unlike the prevailing winds, local winds are not constant; their strength and even their direction may vary widely. For some winds, such as the mistral and the chinook, the surface features of the land explain these variations. For others, such as sea breezes and valley winds, differences in temperature between day and night are the most important factor.

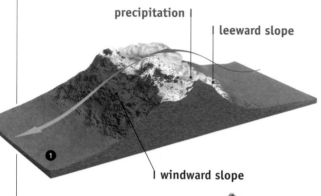

precipitation | leeward slope

windward slope

### THE INFLUENCE OF THE RELIEF

The chinook, which descends the Rocky Mountains in North America, and the foehn, which blows in Switzerland and Austria, are **adiabatic winds ❶**. When air meets the windward slope of a mountain, it rises, cools, and discharges its humidity. After crossing the summit, it warms up as it descends, bringing warm, dry weather to the leeward slope.

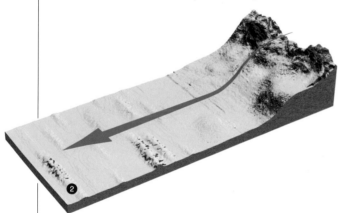

**Katabatic winds ❷** are cold winds that become very strong as they descend mountains. The williwaw in Alaska; the bora, which blows down the Yugoslav mountains toward the Adriatic coast; and the Japanese oroshi are all katabatic winds. The mistral, a dry, cold wind that blows for more than 100 days per year in southeast France, starts in the peaks of the Alps. As the mistral wind descends toward the Rhône Valley, it strengthens, reaching up to 110 mph (180 km/h) by the time it arrives at the Mediterranean Sea.

### THE BEAUFORT SCALE

Developed in 1805 by English admiral Sir Francis Beaufort (1774–1857), the Beaufort scale expresses the strength of the wind according to its effects on the sea. Today, anemometers measure wind speed precisely, and, therefore, correspondences with the Beaufort scale can be established. The strongest surface wind ever, at 230 mph (371 km/h), was measured in 1934 on Mount Washington, in the United States. On the George V coast, in Antarctica, the average winds blow at speeds of about 200 mph (320 km/h).

| force | 0 | 1 | 2 | 3 | 4 | 5 |
|---|---|---|---|---|---|---|
| wind speed | <1 mph (<2 km/h) | 1 to 3 (2 to 6) | 4 to 7 (7 to 11) | 8 to 12 (12 to 19) | 13 to 18 (20 to 29) | 19 to 24 (30 to 39) |
| description | calm | very light breeze | light breeze | gentle breeze | moderate breeze | fresh breeze |

## SEA BREEZE AND LAND BREEZE

In coastal areas, where land and water sit side by side, thermal changes influence the direction of winds.

The **sea breeze ❶** blows during the day, when warm continental air rises, creating a low-pressure zone, which is filled by cool sea air.

At night, when water cools more slowly than land, the reverse phenomenon is produced. Warm air that rises over the sea is replaced by cool land air, creating a **land breeze ❷**.

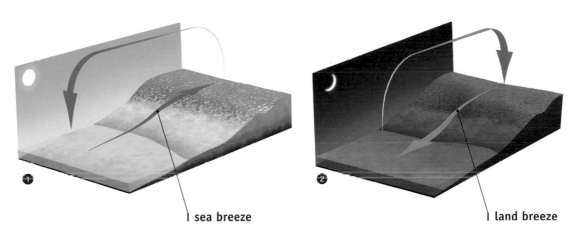

| sea breeze                                    | land breeze

## VALLEY WIND AND MOUNTAIN WIND

A similar phenomenon is produced in mountainous regions, where the temperature change is caused by the difference in altitude between the mountain slopes and the valley floor.

The **valley wind ❶** occurs during the day, when cool valley air is sucked toward higher altitudes, where heating has produced a low-pressure zone.

During the night, the opposite occurs; the **mountain wind ❷** descends toward the valley, where the air has cooled less than in the mountains.

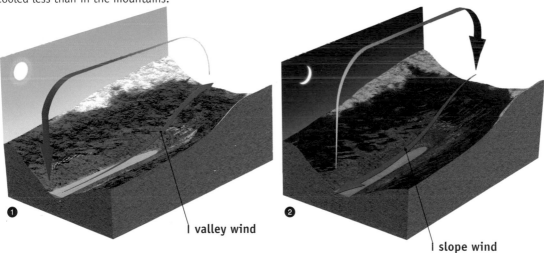

| valley wind                                   | slope wind

| 6 | 7 | 8 | 9 | 10 | 11 | 12 |
|---|---|---|---|---|---|---|
| 25 to 31 (40 to 50) | 32 to 38 (51 to 61) | 39 to 46 (62 to 74) | 47 to 54 (75 to 87) | 55 to 63 (88 to 101) | 64 to 74 (102 to 120) | >74 mph (>120 km/h) |
| strong breeze | near gale | fresh gale | strong gale | whole gale | violent storm | hurricane |

# Tornadoes

## *The most violent winds on Earth*

Tornadoes result from the circling of ascending winds around an intense low-pressure zone. They are notable for their short duration—usually only a few minutes—and for the violence of the winds they generate. These destructive local phenomena usually develop over land with very little warning. Because the mechanisms that lead to their formation are still not well understood, it is difficult for scientists to predict where they will develop.

The **funnel cloud**, an extension of a cloud spinning at the base of a cumulonimbus cloud, is often the first indication that a tornado is forming.

The **diameter** of a tornado varies from 320 to 2,000 feet (100 to 600 m). The funnel may be over a mile (km) high.

Whriling funnel clouds that form over oceans are called **waterspouts**. Although less violent than tornadoes, they are just as spectacular, drawing a funnel of water up to a height of several hundred feet (m).

The **vortex** may be white, gray, brown, black, or even red, depending on the kind of debris sucked up by the tornado and the amount of available sunlight.

The very low pressure within a tornado creates extremely strong **winds**; spikes of over 318 mph (512 km/h) were observed by radar in Oklahoma City in 1999.

The violent winds at the base of the tornado form a **debris cloud.**

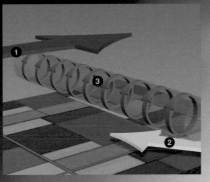 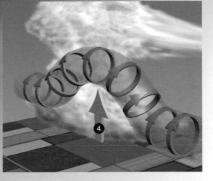

## HOW A TORNADO FORMS

When a cold, strong high-altitude wind ❶ meets a warm, slow surface wind ❷, the air begins to rotate horizontally ❸. If this meeting of shearing winds takes place in a storm cloud, the updraft of warm air ❹ in the storm pushes the rotating tube of air into a vertical position.

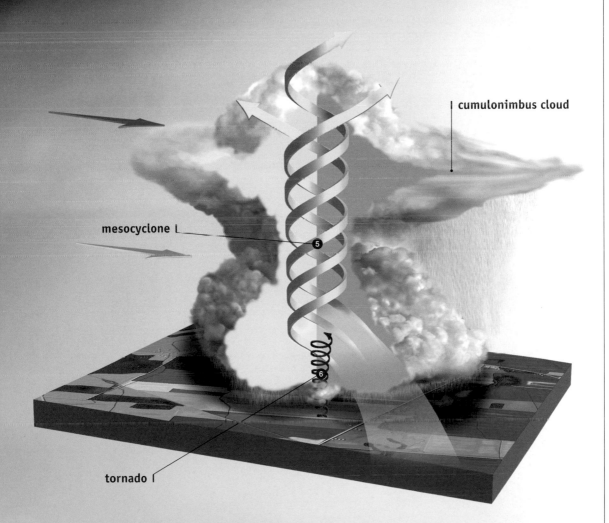

cumulonimbus cloud

mesocyclone

tornado

The combination of ascending and gyrating movement creates a very large column of turbulent air, a mesocyclone ❺. For reasons that are not yet well understood, the spinning air sometimes stretches vertically and a vortex ❻ appears within the mesocyclone. This vortex, which becomes visible if the air is humid enough for condensation, stretches downward until it reaches the ground. When the vortex of a mesocylone touches the ground, it is called a tornado.

# The Power of Tornadoes

*The damage they do*

Although tornadoes are usually very localized and short-lived, their violence makes them particularly dangerous and destructive. Most tornadoes occur in North America, where there are an average of 750 per year, but they also touch down in Europe, Asia, and Australia regularly. In 1925, nearly 700 people died as seven tornadoes traveled over 430 miles (700 km) across parts of the Midwest.

## THE AMERICAN PLAINS: THE HOT SPOT FOR TORNADOES

Most of the tornadoes in North America occur in the central United States, in a "tornado belt" comprising the states of Texas, Oklahoma, Kansas, and Nebraska. In this region, the combination of warm winds from the Gulf of Mexico and cold winds from Canada creates ideal conditions for the formation of mesocyclones, especially in April and May. In the southeastern United States, covering Florida, Alabama, Louisiana, and Mississippi, tornado season occurs earlier, between January and March. The western United States, protected by the Rocky Mountains, is practically tornado-free.

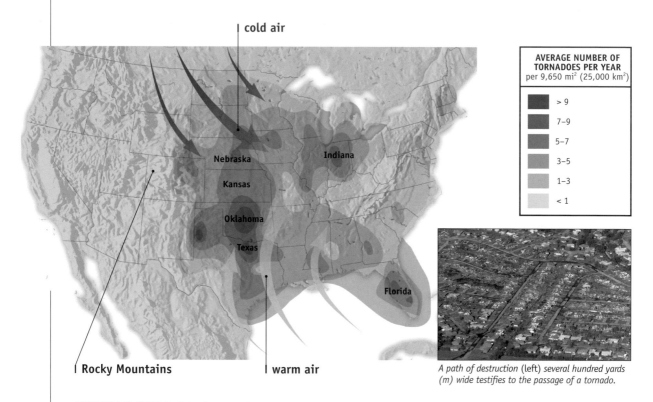

cold air

Nebraska

Indiana

Kansas

Oklahoma

Texas

Florida

Rocky Mountains

warm air

**AVERAGE NUMBER OF TORNADOES PER YEAR**
per 9,650 mi² (25,000 km²)

| | |
|---|---|
| | > 9 |
| | 7–9 |
| | 5–7 |
| | 3–5 |
| | 1–3 |
| | < 1 |

*A path of destruction* (left) *several hundred yards (m) wide testifies to the passage of a tornado.*

## THE TRAJECTORY OF TORNADOES

The path of a tornado depends not on the relief of the land but on how quickly the storm is moving and the position of the vortex in relation to the cloud. A tornado that forms in the center of a mesocyclone takes a straight path ❶ in a rapidly moving storm, but it travels in loops ❷ in a slower-moving storm. Tornadoes that develop on the periphery of a cloud last a shorter time, but they may be followed by several other tornadoes, leaving numerous short paths of damage ❸.

## THE FUJITA SCALE

The suddenness and brief duration of tornadoes make scientific observation of them difficult. Because traditional anemometers cannot withstand the winds that accompany the strongest tornadoes, scientists sometimes have to be content with after-the-fact analysis of the damage caused to evaluate the violence of a tornado. Recently doppler radars have been used to measure wind speeds of tornadoes from a safe distance. The Fujita scale classifies tornadoes in six categories according to the degree of damage caused by the wind speed. The least violent three categories account for 88 percent of observed tornadoes, while the much rarer and most dangerous F5 tornadoes represent only 1 percent of cases.

With winds blowing at less than 73 mph (120 km/h), an **F0 tornado** causes only minor damage, such as broken tree branches and twisted television antennas.

An **F1 tornado**, characterized by winds blowing at speeds of 73 to about 112 mph (120 to 180 km/h), can uproot small trees, turn over trailers, and lift shingles off houses.

The winds in an **F2 tornado** reach between about 113 and 157 mph (180 and 250 km/h) and are capable of destroying wooden structures, moving small vehicles, and knocking over mature trees.

With winds of between 158 and 206 mph (250 and 330 km/h), an **F3 tornado** can knock over large vehicles. Walls collapse and objects weighing several pounds are carried to a high altitude, where they become projectiles.

An **F4 tornado** (winds of 207 to 260 mph [330 to 420 km/h]) destroys solid houses, lifts vehicles, and throws objects weighing well over 200 pounds (100 kg).

An **F5 tornado** is the most violent kind. Its winds of over 260 mph (420 km/h) destroy all types of vehicles and structures in its path.

Whether it is in a solid, liquid, or gaseous state, water is an essential component of Earth's atmosphere. It is constantly moving, changing state, and transporting great quantities of energy all around Earth as it is evaporated by heat, driven by winds, and condensed by cold. Water also gives rise to many spectacular weather phenomena, from snow to rainbows, fog, hail, and hurricanes.

# Precipitation

# Humidity

Water is very widespread on Earth; with a volume of 326 million cubic miles (1,360 million cubic kilometers), it forms almost .2 percent of the planet's total volume. In a gaseous form, it is also found in abundance in the atmosphere. Humidity, or water vapor contained in the air, comes mainly from evaporation of the oceans and transpiration by plants. Its quantity varies widely around the planet, but it is never entirely absent, even in the driest deserts.

### ICE, WATER, AND WATER VAPOR

Like all substances, water can exist in three different states—as a solid, as a liquid, or as a gas—depending on pressure and temperature. At normal atmospheric pressure at sea level (1,013 hPa [14.7 lb/in$^2$]), liquid water solidifies as ice at 32°F (0°C) and vaporizes into an invisible gas, water vapor, at 212°F (100°C).

In its solid state ❶, the water molecules are very strongly linked to each other and form hexagonal crystals. In liquid water ❷, the molecules move not quickly enough to fly apart, but too quickly to form crystals. Water molecules in a gaseous state ❸ are so agitated that they do not stay linked to each other.

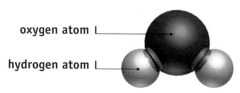

oxygen atom

hydrogen atom

A **water molecule** ($H_2O$) is composed of two hydrogen atoms and one oxygen atom.

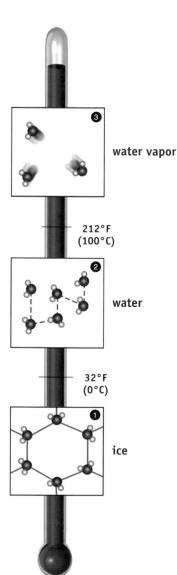

water vapor

212°F (100°C)

water

32°F (0°C)

ice

**THE THREE STATES OF WATER**

### WATER EVAPORATION

Water can be transformed into water vapor at temperatures much lower than 212°F (100°C). In the process called evaporation, molecules on the surface of water absorb thermal energy, become agitated, fly apart, and vaporize. Water can only evaporate if the air is dry enough to absorb new molecules of water vapor.

air free of visible moisture

water

**Evaporation** of water molecules depends on the temperature, pressure, and atmospheric humidity.

### SATURATION OF THE AIR

When the air can absorb no more water vapor, it is said to be saturated. The amount of water vapor air can hold depends on its temperature; warm air can hold more humidity than cold air. If the temperature of saturated air drops, some of the water vapor it contains returns to a liquid state through a process called condensation. The temperature at which an air mass is saturated is called the dew point.

saturated air

When the air is saturated, **condensation** compensates for evaporation.

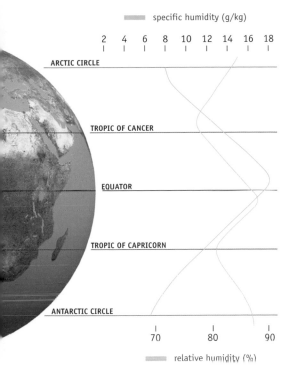

specific humidity (g/kg)

2  4  6  8  10  12  14  16  18

ARCTIC CIRCLE

TROPIC OF CANCER

EQUATOR

TROPIC OF CAPRICORN

ANTARCTIC CIRCLE

70        80        90

relative humidity (%)

## SPECIFIC HUMIDITY AND RELATIVE HUMIDITY

**Specific humidity** expresses the exact weight of water vapor contained in the air. It is a very stable quantity, since the weight of a substance does not vary with temperature or pressure. On the other hand, specific humidity cannot indicate the relationship between temperature and humidity, which is behind many weather phenomena.

**Relative humidity** expresses the relationship between the quantity of water vapor contained in an air mass and the quantity necessary to saturate that air mass. Saturated air has 100 percent relative humidity, while totally dry air, which does not exist, would have a relative humidity of 0 percent. Since saturation depends on the temperature, the relative humidity is higher near the poles than in tropical regions.

## HOW WE FEEL HUMIDITY

Because it impedes perspiration, high humidity is perceived by the human body as a heat-aggravating factor. The sensible temperature, meaning how humans perceive the combination of temperature and humidity, is obtained by combining the real temperature and the relative humidity.

| SENSIBLE TEMPERATURE | |
|---|---|
| | Extreme heat<br>Imminent heat stroke |
| | High heat<br>Cramps, risk of heat stroke, and exhaustion |
| | Moderate heat<br>Cramps and exhaustion possible |
| | Slight heat<br>Discomfort |

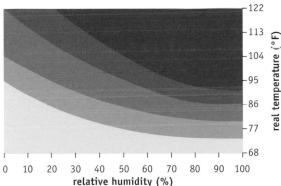

real temperature (°F)

122 — 113 — 104 — 95 — 86 — 77 — 68

0  10  20  30  40  50  60  70  80  90  100

relative humidity (%)

**❶**

**❷**

## VAPOR AND CLOUDS AROUND EARTH

Water vapor is invisible, but the infrared rays detected by the many weather satellites reveal how it is distributed in Earth's atmosphere ❶. On the other hand, water is visible in its liquid state. In the visible spectrum ❷, the satellites can observe clouds, which are made of droplets of water.

# Clouds

## Huge water reservoirs

Contrary to popular belief, clouds are not made mainly of water vapor but of billions of tiny—less than .0008 inches (.02 millimeters) in diameter—water droplets and ice crystals. Although these particles are too light to fall to the ground, they nevertheless constitute a colossal mass of water—over 550,000 tons (500,000 metric tons) in a cumulonimbus cloud. For a cloud to form, humid air must be cooled to the temperature at which the water vapor it contains condenses. A number of different atmospheric phenomena can cause warm air masses to rise and, consequently, to cool.

### CONDENSATION NUCLEI

Condensation of water vapor is caused by cooling of the air mass that contains it. This transformation occurs, however, only if water molecules come into contact with condensation nuclei, or solids to which they can attach themselves. Dust, volcanic ash, pollen grains, and salt crystals in suspension in the atmosphere can play this role.

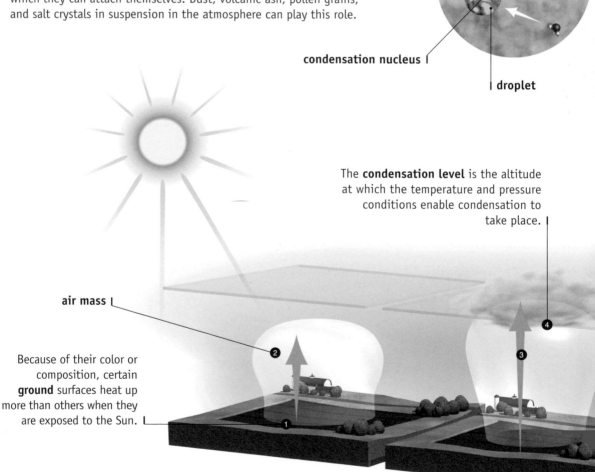

water molecule

condensation nucleus

droplet

The **condensation level** is the altitude at which the temperature and pressure conditions enable condensation to take place.

air mass

Because of their color or composition, certain **ground** surfaces heat up more than others when they are exposed to the Sun.

### CONVECTION CLOUDS

The ground ❶ heated by the Sun transmits its heat to the air above it, which creates a mass of warm air ❷. This mass, lighter than the air around it, rises rapidly ❸. As it moves upward, it cools until it reaches its dew point, or the temperature at which the air is saturated with humidity, at an altitude called its condensation level ❹. The moisture in the air mass condenses and forms a cumulus cloud ❺. This cloud is pushed by the wind ❻ and may grow as it passes over other rising air masses ❼.

## OROGRAPHIC CLOUDS

When a humid air mass meets a geographic feature, such as a mountain, that forces it to rise above the condensation level, the moisture that it contains condenses and an orographic cloud, or "mountain cloud," forms. This phenomenon is often accompanied by precipitation, and the slope on the other side of the mountain is generally quite dry.

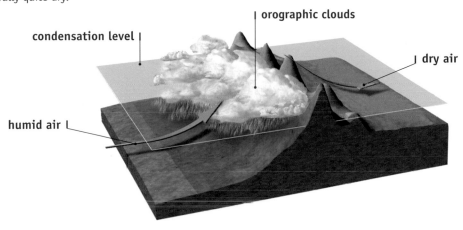

condensation level

orographic clouds

dry air

humid air

## FRONTAL CLOUDS

The collision of two air masses with different temperatures forces the warmer air to rise along the front, which causes a cloud to form.

frontal clouds

condensation level

cool air

warm air

front

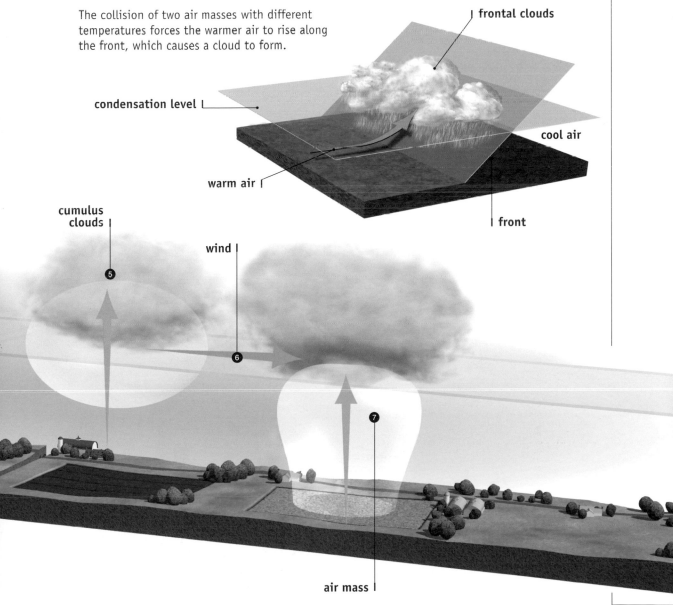

cumulus clouds

wind

air mass

# Identifying Clouds

*Indicators of atmospheric activity*

In spite of their apparently wide variety, clouds can be grouped into four families and 10 main types, based on their altitude and shape. This classification, invented in 1807 by the English naturalist Luke Howard (1772–1864), enables us not only to identify clouds, but also to understand how atmospheric conditions evolve and, sometimes, to forecast the weather.

## CLOUDS OF VERTICAL DEVELOPMENT

Although their flattened bases are located at low altitudes between 1,650 feet and 6,560 feet (500 m and 2,000 m), cumulus and cumulonimbus clouds may extend several miles (km) in height because of the powerful updrafts that rise through them.

**Cumulonimbus** clouds are the most impressive. While their very dark-colored bases are just above the ground, their tops may rise to the tropopause, more than 49,000 feet (15,000 m) in altitude. Swept by strong winds at a very high altitude, they widen into their characteristic anvil shape. Thunderstorms, heavy showers, hail, and even violent tornadoes often develop in them.

Dense, white, fluffy **cumulus** clouds are formed by convection, usually during a warm summer day. Associated with stable good weather, they form showers only if their vertical development is very high.

## THREE STAGES OF CLOUDS

Cirrus, cirrocumulus, and cirrostratus clouds are **high-altitude clouds** (above 19,600 feet [6,000 m]) composed of ice crystals. Generally thin and white, they do not generate precipitation themselves but indicate the arrival of a cyclone when they thicken.

**Medium-altitude clouds** (from 6,550 feet to 19,700 feet [2,000 m to 6,000 m]) are made up of a mixture of water droplets and ice crystals. They are divided into altostratus and altocumulus clouds.

**Low-altitude clouds, such as** nimbostratus, stratocumulus, and stratus clouds, whose bases have altitiudes no higher than 6,560 feet (2,000 m), are formed of water droplets, sometimes mixed with ice crystals. Their appearance, which generally corresponds to the passing of a cyclone, causes continuous precipitation in the form of rain or snow, depending on the season.

**49,000 feet (15,000 m) –**

**Cirrocumulus** clouds are made up of small granular or rippled masses that can be arranged in rows.

**Cirrus** clouds, which look stringy or feathery, are the most common high clouds.

**Cirrostratus** clouds, often covering much of the sky in the form of an almost transparent veil, create a halo around the Sun.

**19,700 feet (6,000 m) –**

**Altocumulus** clouds form as banks of small, white or gray clouds, spread out in a regular pattern and sometimes in parallel rows. If these small masses get closer together, they indicate the arrival of a low pressure zone, or cyclone.

**Altostratus** clouds form dark, gray or bluish layers of varying thickness and are capable of dropping large amounts of precipitation.

**Nimbostratus** clouds, identified by their gray layers with poorly defined contours, provide continuous precipitation.

**6,550 feet (2,000 m) –**

**Stratocumulus** clouds consist of banks of gray, sometimes dark gray, clouds. Despite their color, they generally are not associated with precipitation.

**Stratus** clouds, which are seen as low, gray, cloudy layers, similar to fog, can cause drizzle, or very light rain.

**0 feet –**

# Precipitation

*Why water falls from the sky*

Every year, the equivalent of over 3 feet (1 m) of water, in various forms, falls to Earth from the sky. This precipitation comes from clouds, where a million droplets must join together to form a single raindrop that is big enough to fight air resistance and fall to the ground. Condensation begins the process, but condensation alone is not enought to lead to this incredible agglomeration. Other mechanisms must come into play.

## RELATIVE SIZES OF DROPS AND DROPLETS

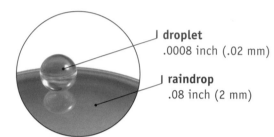

droplet
.0008 inch (.02 mm)

raindrop
.08 inch (2 mm)

## RAIN FROM WARM CLOUDS

The humidity in rising air condenses in the form of droplets ❶. When these grow to a certain size through coalescence, they begin to sink ❷, then fall as rain ❸. If updrafts ❹ are strong, the forming drops remain in the cloud longer. As they fall ❺, they grow larger ❻.

## COALESCENCE

Droplets that reach diameters of about .001 inch (.05 mm) to .004 inch (.1 mm) through condensation begin to drop slowly through the cloud. As they fall, they get bigger by taking on the droplets with which they collide. When a drop reaches about .25 inch (6 mm) in diameter, air pressure breaks it into several smaller drops.

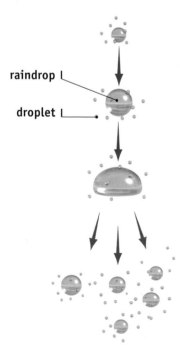

raindrop

droplet

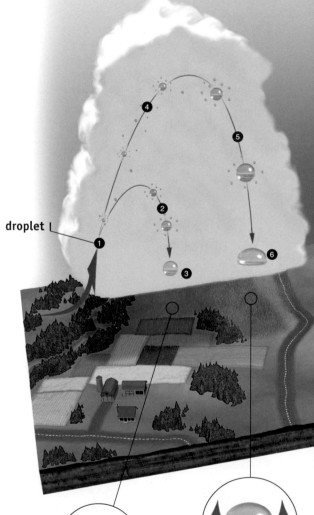

droplet

The shape of a **raindrop** depends on its size. Drops that are less than .08 inch (2 mm) in diameter are spherical, while larger ones flatten out due to the force of air pressure.

## RAIN AND SNOW IN COLD CLOUDS

Droplets of supercooled water, or water that remains in a liquid state at temperatures below 32°F (0°C), ❶ are transformed into ice crystals ❷ when they collide with particles in suspension in the air. The surrounding water vapor freezes onto these crystals, changing their shapes ❸ and making them heavier. If they enter a warmer air mass as they fall, they melt ❹ into raindrops ❺. If the air temperature remains under 32°F (0°C), the crystals fall as snow ❻.

## FORMATION OF HAILSTONES

The "embryo" of a hailstone is made of a droplet that freezes ❶ as it is pushed by the powerful updrafts of up to 62 mph (100 km/h) that rise through a cumulonimbus cloud during a storm. As it drops again toward the lower, more humid parts of the cloud, this "embryo" is covered with a layer of transparent ice ❷ made up of droplets from the surrounding cloud. Once again propelled upward by updrafts, the hailstone rises toward colder air masses, where a new layer of ice, this one opaque, increases its size ❸. The hailstone travels up and down in the cloud many times ❹, each time adding transparent and opaque layers alternately, until its weight makes it drop ❺ toward the ground at speeds of up to 100 mph (160 km/h).

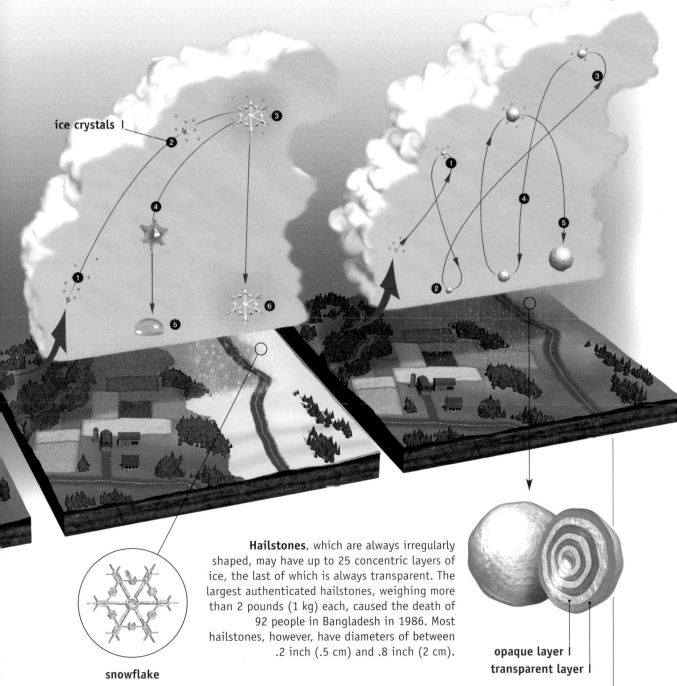

ice crystals

**Hailstones**, which are always irregularly shaped, may have up to 25 concentric layers of ice, the last of which is always transparent. The largest authenticated hailstones, weighing more than 2 pounds (1 kg) each, caused the death of 92 people in Bangladesh in 1986. Most hailstones, however, have diameters of between .2 inch (.5 cm) and .8 inch (2 cm).

snowflake

opaque layer
transparent layer

# Types of Precipitation
## *Between the clouds and the ground*

Precipitation takes both liquid and solid forms. Depending on the thickness of the clouds, their humidity level, the temperature of the ambient air, and the ground temperature, precipitation can form as drizzle, raindrops, ice pellets, or snow.

## DIFFERENT FORMS OF RAIN

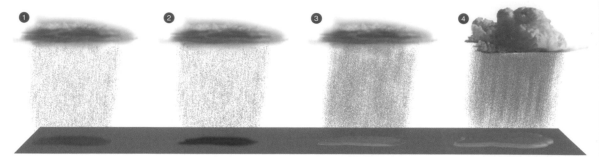

**Drizzle ❶**, formed of very small raindrops less than .02 inch (.5 mm) in diameter, comes from low clouds, such as stratus clouds, and leads to very little accumulation at ground level.

Rain made up of larger drops .02 to .2 inch (.5 to 5 mm) in diameter is classified according to the quantity of precipitation that it produces within a defined time period. **Light rain ❷** leaves less than one inch (25 mm) of water on the ground per hour; **moderate rain ❸**, from one to three inches (25 to 76 mm); and **heavy rain ❹**, more than three inches (76 mm). While steady rain usually comes from thick clouds, such as nimbostratus clouds, showers, or brief, sudden, heavy rains, usually form in cumulonimbus clouds.

## WINTER PRECIPITATION

Although snow is often associated with winter, it is not the only type of winter precipitation. As snowflakes pass through the air masses that separate the clouds from the ground, they heat up or cool down, thus undergoing transformations that determine the final form of the precipitation.

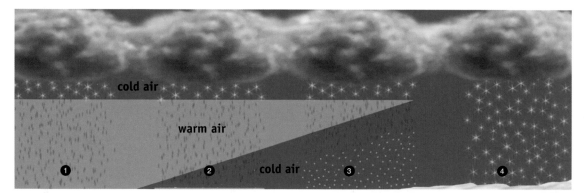

cold air

warm air

cold air

When the air temperature is above the freezing point, the snowflakes produced by the cloud melt and fall in the form of **rain ❶**.

If the raindrops travel through a thin layer of cold air, they become supercooled, or cooled below the freezing point but remaining in liquid form. On impact, they freeze instantly and form a slick glaze of ice. This type of precipitation is called **freezing rain ❷**.

Passing through a thin layer of warm air partially melts snowflakes. Their surfaces freeze again as they move through a new layer of cold air; they become small bits of ice (.2 inch [5 mm]) known as **ice pellets ❸**.

If the snowflakes do not pass through a warm air mass, they do not melt, and **snow ❹** accumulates on the ground.

## CRYSTAL SHAPES DEPEND ON THE TEMPERATURE

Snowflakes are the result of an aggregation of thousands of ice crystals whose size and variety of shapes, including platelet, needle, column, and star, depend on air temperature and humidity.

32°F (0°C)

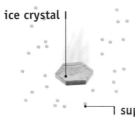

platelet

27°F (-3°C)

needle

21°F (-6°C)

column

14°F (-10°C)

sector plate

10°F (-12°C)

star

-3°F (16°C)

sector plate

-8°F (-22°C)

column

## HOW A SNOWFLAKE IS FORMED

In clouds, ice crystals grow by absorbing surrounding water molecules. When they are heavy enough, they fall.

ice crystal

supercooled water droplet

When supercooled water droplets are hit by an ice crystal, they freeze instantly and stick to it in a process called **accretion**.

The crystals that **collide** break into many small ice particles, which grow, in turn, through accretion.

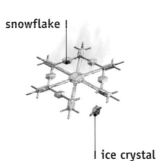

snowflake

ice crystal

If the air humidity is high and the temperature is near 32°F (0°C), the ice crystals stick to each other and form more complex structures, snowflakes, which can reach over an inch (cm) in diameter. The process of crystals sticking together is called **aggregation**.

## EVERY SNOWFLAKE IS DIFFERENT

Although they have an almost infinite variety of forms, all snowflakes are hexagonal because of the molecular structure of the water from which they are made. Because snowflakes are brittle and often combine with other falling crystals, their shapes look like natural works of art.

33

# Dew and Fog

## The ground's influence

Not all meteorological phenomena are produced at high altitudes. In fact, the temperature of the ground sometimes causes atmospheric humidity to condense, and water droplets of various sizes appear on or just above the terrain.

### DEW AND FROST

In the early morning, grass and objects close to the ground are sometimes covered with water droplets or a fine layer of white ice. These phenomena, which are linked to the temperature and relative humidity of the air, usually take place in clear, mild weather. They therefore cannot come from clouds.

**Dew** appears when the ground cools to the dew point, or the temperature at which the air is saturated with water vapor. The water molecules contained in the surrounding layer of air condense once in contact with cold surfaces, forming drops about .04 inch (1 mm) in diameter.

If the dew point is below 32°F (0°C), the vapor does not condense in dewdrops but is transformed directly into ice crystals, or **frost**. Frost is not the same thing as frozen dew, which occurs when the soil cools to below the freezing point after the dew has formed.

### FOG AND MIST: CLOUDS JUST ABOVE THE GROUND

Like all other types of clouds, **fog** forms by condensation of water vapor contained in air. Usually, radiation fog is caused by nighttime cooling of the ground, when the ground radiates its heat out to space. It can reduce visibility to .6 mile (1 km) or less and sometimes to just a few yards (m).

When the droplets are more dispersed, fog is called **mist**. Visibility is limited to between .6 and 3 miles (1 and 5 km).

# Rainbows

## Colors in the sky

Although the Sun's light usually appears white, it is in fact composed of the range of colors that correspond to different wavelengths—red, orange, yellow, green, blue, indigo, and violet. It is these components of the spectrum of light that appear when the Sun illuminates a curtain of raindrops. The higher the Sun is in the sky, the lower the rainbow is on the horizon. Therefore, natural rainbows are only visible at the beginning and end of the day.

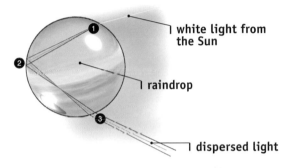

white light from the Sun

raindrop

dispersed light

### HOW RAIN DISPERSES LIGHT

When a sunbeam penetrates a raindrop, it refracts ❶, or changes direction. The back of the drop reflects ❷ this light and refracts it again before it leaves the raindrop ❸.

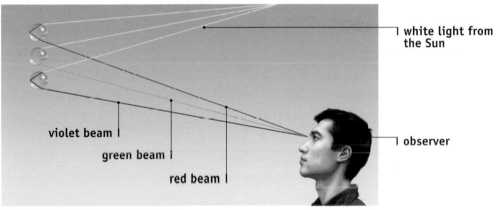

white light from the Sun

violet beam

green beam

red beam

observer

Each wavelength has a different angle of refraction. White light from the Sun is dispersed by each raindrop into beams of colored light that contain the entire visible spectrum, from red to violet. We actually see only one color per raindrop, but the huge number of drops, each acting as a tiny prism, forms the range of colors that we perceive, a **rainbow**.

### DOUBLE RAINBOW

Sometimes, two reflections occur within a single raindrop. In these cases, a secondary rainbow, less sharply defined and with the colors in reverse order, then appears over the first one.

secondary rainbow

primary rainbow

# Thunderstorms

## Abounding energy

With heavy rain, violent winds, lightning, thunder, hail, and even tornadoes, approximately 50,000 thunderstorms occur in Earth's atmosphere every day. Each storm unleashes the energy equivalent to that of an atom bomb. Thunderstorms are very common in the intertropical zones, and they also occur in temperate zones in spring and summer, when the ingredients necessary to form a thunderstorm—warm, humid air and instability—are more frequently present.

### HOW TO RECOGNIZE A GROWING CUMULUS CLOUD

When the top of a cloud reflects the Sun's rays, it is because it is loaded with water droplets. This condition indicates the presence of strong warm updrafts, which cause cumulus clouds to become cumulonimbus clouds—the kind likely to produce a thunderstorm.

The predominance of ice crystals, which let the Sun's rays partially through, in contrast, is the mark of a cumulus cloud that has finished growing.

cumulus cloud

②

①

development phase

## THE LIFE CYCLE OF A THUNDERSTORM CELL

The life cycle of a thunderstorm cell has three stages. In the development stage, the updraft ❶ of a humid air mass, either by convection or due to the arrival of a cold front, forms a cumulus cloud ❷. If the air is unstable, warm currents ❸ continue to rise, and the cloud grows to the cumulonimbus stage ❹. When it reaches the tropopause, the cloud stops developing in height and becomes loaded with ice crystals that begin the precipitation process. The thunderstorm then enters its mature stage, as the cold, heavy air from the top of the cloud suddenly falls in strong currents ❺ accompanied by thunder, lightning ❻, and heavy showers ❼. The thunderstorm dissipates when the winds ❽ from the top of the cloud cool the ground to the point where the cloud is deprived of the warm air that was feeding it. The cumulonimbus cloud disintegrates, the rain stops, and only a few inoffensive cirrus and altocumulus clouds remain in the sky.

The entire cycle lasts no more than an hour, but winds that continue to propagate after the storm dissipates may encounter new warm, humid air masses, triggering the formation of a new storm cell. When a chain of storm cells occurs, it is called a multicell storm.

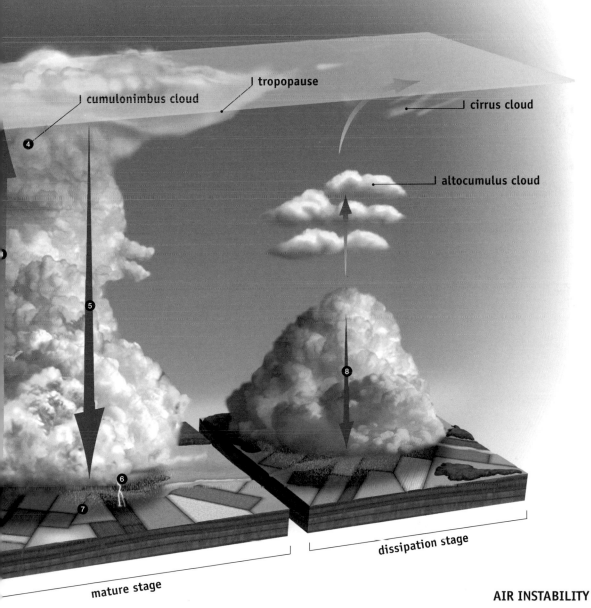

tropopause

cumulonimbus cloud

cirrus cloud

altocumulus cloud

dissipation stage

mature stage

### AIR INSTABILITY

Since air pressure decreases with increasing altitude, a rising air parcel undergoes adiabatic cooling, or cooling due to expansion, of almost 2°F (1°C) every 330 feet (100 m) or so. If the temperature of the air surrounding the rising parcel drops more rapidly than the rising parcel itself, the air is called unstable. The air parcel, which is warmer than the surrounding air, continues to rise. If the air in the parcel is humid, the condensing water liberates heat, which causes additional rising.

# Lightning and Thunder
## *Electricity in the air*

Every second, several hundred lightning flashes crackle around the planet. These giant sparks are due to electrical discharges called strikes, which are produced during the mature phase of a thunderstorm. This spectacular phenomenon can also be very dangerous. With their electrical currents on the order of 100,000 amperes, lightning strikes cause the deaths of hundreds of people every year. They are also responsible for many fires, short circuits, and electrical outages, as well as electromagnetic interference.

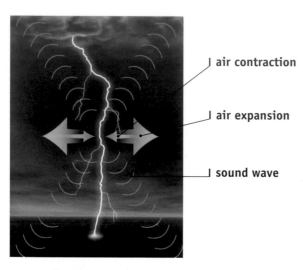

air contraction

air expansion

sound wave

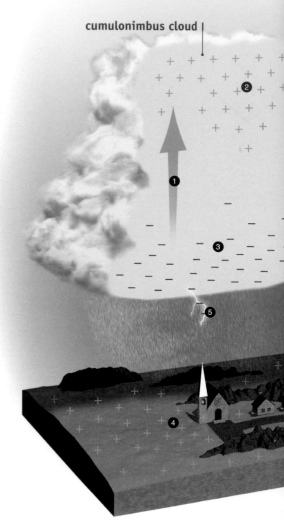

cumulonimbus cloud

### FROM STRIKE TO THUNDER

As it is transmitted to the surrounding air, the 54,000°F (30,000°C) heat of a strike causes the air to suddenly expand and contract. These movements create a shock wave that makes a booming sound—thunder.

When shock waves from different parts of the lightning strike reach us at different times, we hear thunder as a prolonged, rumbling sound.

### THUNDER DELAYED

We see a lightning flash almost the instant it occurs, but the sound of thunder takes longer to reach us because sound travels more slowly than light. If we count the number of seconds in the delay and divide it by 5 (3), we can estimate our distance in miles (km) from the site where the strike occurred.

## HOW A LIGHTNING FLASH FORMS BETWEEN A CLOUD AND THE GROUND

By a process that is not yet fully understood, air currents ❶ distribute positive charges ❷ to the top of a cumulonimbus cloud and negative charges ❸ to its base. The ground under the cloud becomes positively charged ❹ in reaction to the cloud. An electrical field is thus created, which grows until the air stops acting as an insulator, as it normally does. An electron flow called the leader ❺, an invisible spark that moves at 125 miles per second (200 km/s) along a jagged path, shoots out of the negatively charged zone. As it approaches the ground, the leader attracts a positive electron flow ❻. When the two sparks meet, they form a channel of ionized air several inches (cm) in diameter along which a very powerful positive current, known as the return stroke, rises ❼. This electrical discharge produces the luminous line of a lightning flash.

Positive charges are concentrated in raised objects which have better electrical conductivity than air, such as structures, trees, life forms, and metallic objects. The **return stroke,** therefore, usually comes from these objects.

## DIFFERENT TYPES OF LIGHTNING

Although these are very spectacular, only 20 percent of all lightning flashes hit the ground ❶. The others are produced between two clouds ❷, within a single cloud ❸, or between a cloud and the surrounding air ❹. Lightning occurring within a cloud is the most common type. All lightning bolts, however, link a negatively charged zone to a positively charged zone, obeying the rule that opposite electrical charges attract.

# The Birth of a Hurricane
## The makings of a giant tropical storm

Names such as Andrew, Hugo, Allen, and Mitch refer to some of the most devastating meteorological phenomena—hurricanes. When they are at their strongest, these giant tropical storms may be accompanied by winds of more than 150 mph (250 km/h). A tropical storm needs only a few ingredients to form: a large mass of warm water, an initial low pressure system (cyclone), and moderate winds blowing in a constant direction.

### HOW A TROPICAL STORM FORMS

When the Sun warms the top layer ❶ of the ocean, strong updrafts of warm, humid air are formed by convection, creating a low-pressure zone ❷. This movement of air provokes the convergence of low-altitude winds ❸, also loaded with humidity, which feed the rising movement ❹. Once in contact with cooler air, the water vapor condenses ❺ and forms a storm cloud. The latent heat ❻, or the heat associated with the change of water between solid, liquid, and gaseous states, released by the condensation accelerates the rising of the air within a column ❼ that sucks up more mid-level warm, humid air ❽. As the atmospheric pressure increases at the top of the cloud, diverging winds ❾ form and the air is expelled. As it descends ❿, the air is heated and sucked in by the surface low-pressure zone.

Constant moderate **winds** at all altitudes impede dispersion of the heat in the forming storm.

To feed the tropical storm, the **ocean surface** must be heated to a temperature of at least 80°F (27°C), down to a depth of at least 230 feet (70 m).

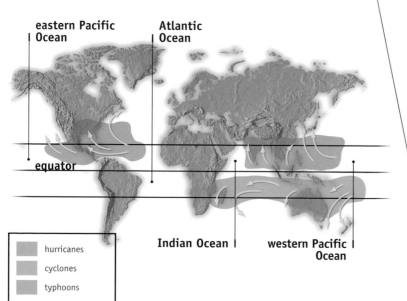

eastern Pacific Ocean

Atlantic Ocean

equator

Indian Ocean

western Pacific Ocean

hurricanes

cyclones

typhoons

### CYCLONE, HURRICANE, OR TYPHOON?

Powerful tropical storms are formed exclusively in the intertropical zone between 5° and 20° latitude on either side of the equator. The same type of storm is called a typhoon in the northwest Pacific Ocean, a hurricane in the North Atlantic and northeast Pacific oceans, and a cyclone in the Indian and southwest Pacific oceans.

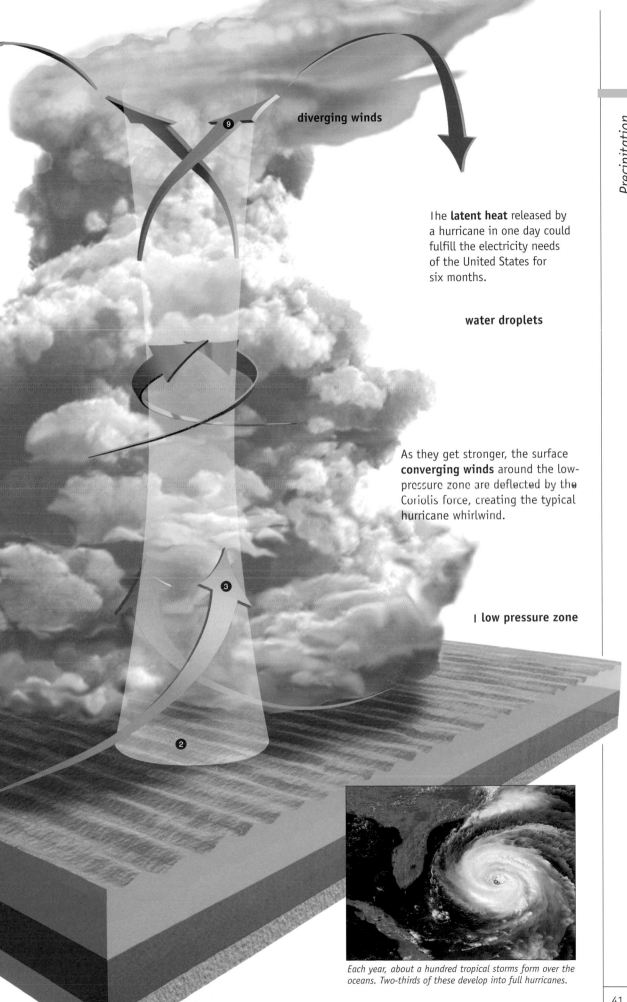

**diverging winds**

The **latent heat** released by a hurricane in one day could fulfill the electricity needs of the United States for six months.

**water droplets**

As they get stronger, the surface **converging winds** around the low-pressure zone are deflected by the Coriolis force, creating the typical hurricane whirlwind.

I **low pressure zone**

*Each year, about a hundred tropical storms form over the oceans. Two-thirds of these develop into full hurricanes.*

# Inside a Hurricane

## *A formidable heat engine*

Hurricanes draw the humid, warm atmosphere and the oceans into a circular movement. This mechanism plays an essential role in the energy balance of the planet, but it is also responsible for the deaths of an average of 20,000 people each year.

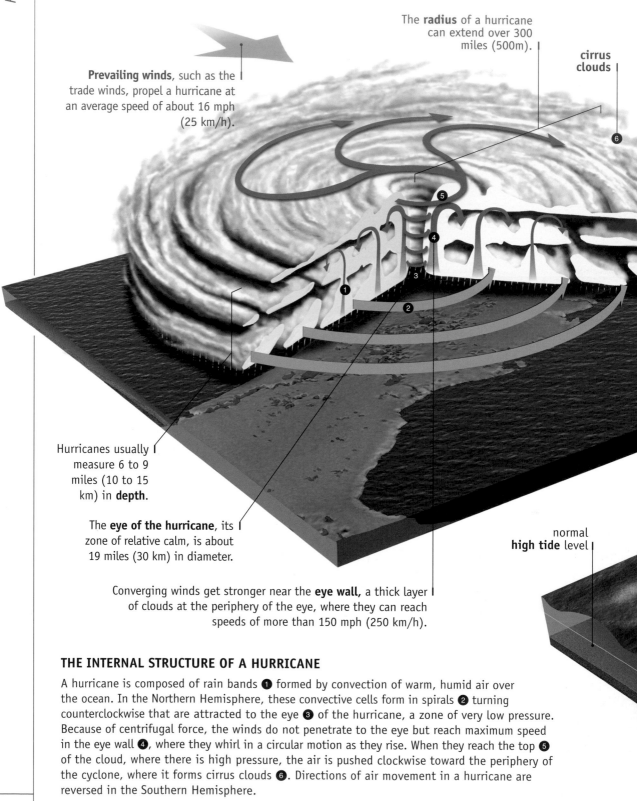

The **radius** of a hurricane can extend over 300 miles (500m).

**cirrus clouds**

**Prevailing winds**, such as the trade winds, propel a hurricane at an average speed of about 16 mph (25 km/h).

Hurricanes usually measure 6 to 9 miles (10 to 15 km) in **depth**.

The **eye of the hurricane**, its zone of relative calm, is about 19 miles (30 km) in diameter.

normal **high tide** level

Converging winds get stronger near the **eye wall,** a thick layer of clouds at the periphery of the eye, where they can reach speeds of more than 150 mph (250 km/h).

## THE INTERNAL STRUCTURE OF A HURRICANE

A hurricane is composed of rain bands ❶ formed by convection of warm, humid air over the ocean. In the Northern Hemisphere, these convective cells form in spirals ❷ turning counterclockwise that are attracted to the eye ❸ of the hurricane, a zone of very low pressure. Because of centrifugal force, the winds do not penetrate to the eye but reach maximum speed in the eye wall ❹, where they whirl in a circular motion as they rise. When they reach the top ❺ of the cloud, where there is high pressure, the air is pushed clockwise toward the periphery of the cyclone, where it forms cirrus clouds ❻. Directions of air movement in a hurricane are reversed in the Southern Hemisphere.

## THE OCEAN SUCKED UP BY THE HURRICANE

Hurricanes are accompanied by an unusual and devastating phenomenon—storm surges. Pushed by violent converging winds and sucked up by the storm cyclone, the ocean surface rises many feet (m) under the eye of the hurricane ❶. When a hurricane reaches a coast, this mass of water floods the shore ❷.

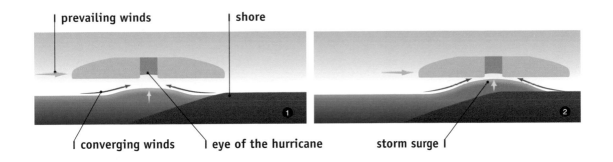

prevailing winds

shore

converging winds

eye of the hurricane

storm surge

## DAMAGE CAUSED BY HURRICANES

The destructive effects of a hurricane are felt when it reaches a coast. Violent winds rip up trees and destroy buildings. Due to torrential rains, rivers rise over their banks and landslides occur. Finally, storm surges cause floods, often with tragic consequences, including massive loss of life. More than 300,000 people drowned during a hurricane in Bangladesh in 1970, when the sea rose about 40 feet (12 m).

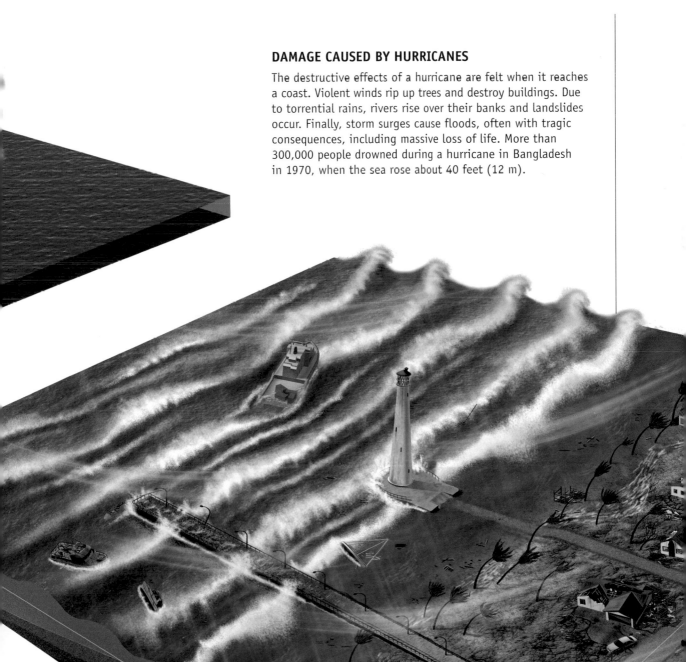

# The Life of a Hurricane
## *An increasingly well-understood phenomenon*

Using satellites, planes, radar, and probes, scientists have been studying hurricanes for 50 years in order to understand how they develop and change, from the initial formation of a tropical low pressure system to the dissipation of the storm. Although the phenomenon of hurricanes is now well understood, it is still impossible to forecast their precise paths several days in advance because they can suddenly change direction or even double back on their path.

### EVOLUTION OF A HURRICANE

When a disturbance becomes organized around a low-pressure zone where winds are blowing at between 23 and 39 mph (37 and 62 km/h), the disturbance is called a **tropical depression** ❶. As the low-pressure zone deepens and winds rise to between 40 and 73 mph (63 and 117 km/h), the tropical depression develops into a **tropical storm** ❷.  A tropical storm becomes a **hurricane** ❸ when wind speeds are above 73 mph (118 km/h). In the eye that forms at the center of the cloud mass, the pressure drops below 980 hPa. The **dissipation stage** ❹ starts just a few hours after the hurricane travels inland. Deprived of its main source of energy, warm water, the storm weakens very quickly.

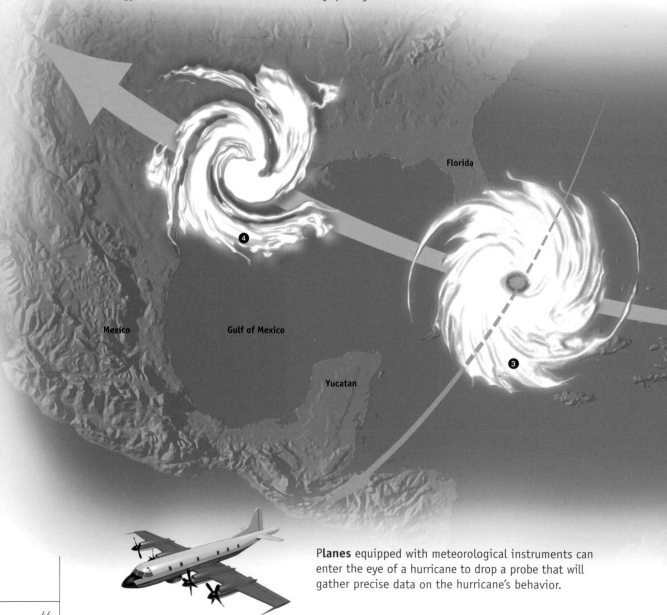

Florida

❹

Mexico

Gulf of Mexico

Yucatan

❸

**Planes** equipped with meteorological instruments can enter the eye of a hurricane to drop a probe that will gather precise data on the hurricane's behavior.

# CLASSIFICATION OF HURRICANES

The Saffir-Simpson scale defines five categories of hurricanes based on atmospheric pressure, wind speed, and the height of the storm surge. The scale allows the amount of damage to be predicted.

| category | 1 | 2 | 3 | 4 | 5 |
|---|---|---|---|---|---|
| pressure | >980 hPa | 965–980 hPa | 945–964 hPa | 920–944 hPa | <920 hPa |
| wind speed | 73-94 mph (118–152 km/h) | 95-109 mph (153–176 km/h) | 110-129 mph (177–208 km/h) | 130-154 mph (209–248 km/h) | >154 mph (>248 km/h) |
| height of surge | 4-5 ft (1.2–1.5 m) | 5-8 ft (1.6–2.4 m) | 8-12 ft (2.5–3.6 m) | 12-18 ft (3.7–5.4 m) | >18 ft (>5.4 m) |

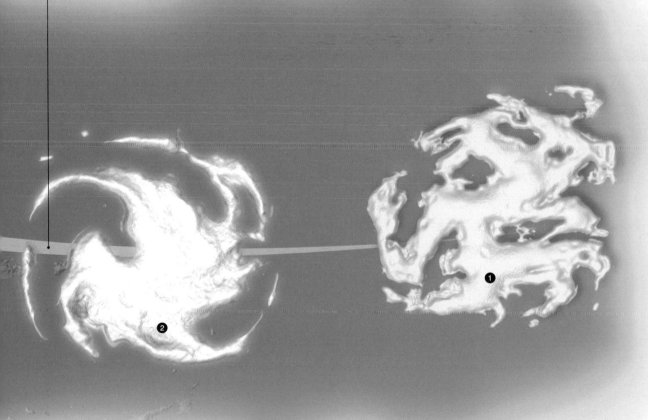

Pushed by the **trade winds**, hurricanes move first from east to west and then tend to move away from the equator. When a hurricane reaches subtropical regions, it encounters western prevailing winds that deflect its path toward the north or northeast (or toward the south or southeast in the Southern Hemisphere). Some may reach latitudes of 40° to 45°.

## NAMING HURRICANES

Tropical storms and hurricanes are given human first names, alternating between male and female names, and running in alphabetical order. The lists of names, prepared in advance by the World Meteorological Organization, are recycled every five years, except for the names of the most destructive storms, which are retired. Thus, Andrew, Gilbert, Hugo, and Allen will never be used again.

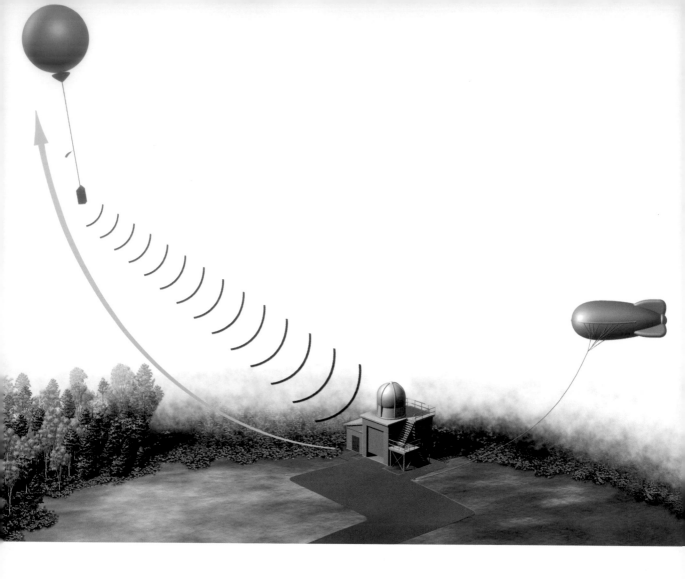

What will the weather be tomorrow? To help answer this question, meteorologists have a vast network of weather observation equipment distributed around the planet and even in space. Day and night, they use measurement instruments to gather data at ground level and on the oceans. At the same time, they use radar, balloons, and satellites to scrutinize the atmosphere, tracking winds, clouds, and precipitation.

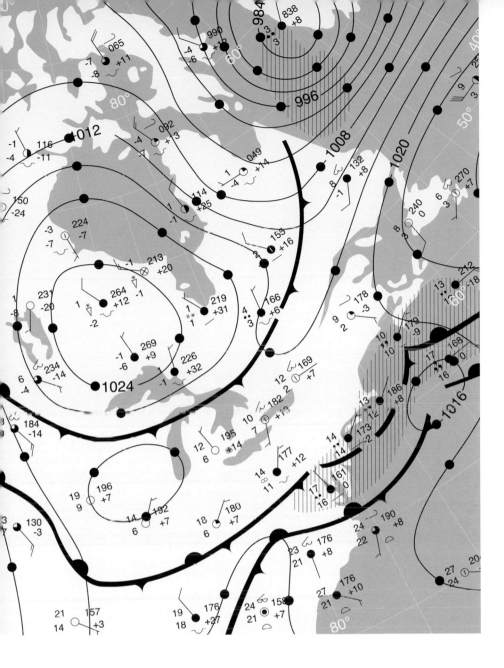

# Meteorology

# Measurement Instruments
## *Gathering meteorological data*

A number of variables, including wind direction and strength, air temperature and humidity, sunshine hours, barometric pressure, and amount of precipitation, are measured daily by 12,000 weather stations spread around Earth. The World Meteorological Organization collects these observations and uses them to create computer models of weather patterns from which weather forecasts are made.

### MEASURING SUNSHINE HOURS

Two different instruments are used to measure the quantity of solar radiation and number of sunshine hours.

The **pyranometer** records diffuse radiation from the sky using a thermopile. It is equipped with a shadow band that blocks direct solar radiation.

The **heliograph** consists of a glass sphere that focuses solar radiation in a manner similar to a magnifying glass. The length of the burn marks left on the graduated chart placed under the sphere indicates when the Sun shines and for how long. It is no longer widely used.

**shadow band**

**glass sphere**

**chart-holder**

**thermopile**

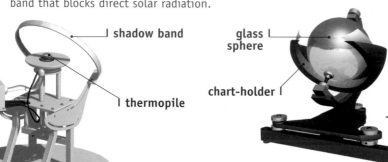

### MEASURING PRECIPITATION

The amount of rainfall is determined by the height of the water that accumulates in a container called a **rain gauge**. Rain is collected through a funnel that directs it into a graduated test tube.

**collection funnel**

**Snow gauges** like this one do not work well, so meteorologists average three measurements taken with yardsticks in different places to estimate snow depth.

**tipping bucket**

A **recorder** notes when the bucket emits an electrical impulse.

The **test tube** of a rain gauge is marked with lines, like those on a ruler, to take account of the relationship between its diameter and that of the instrument's funnel.

The **pluviograph** records the amount of rain that falls throughout a day. Also called the "tipping bucket rain gauge," it emits a signal and empties its contents into a receptacle when the weight of the gathered water tips it.

## MEASURING AIR PRESSURE

The standard instrument for measuring atmospheric pressure is the **mercury barometer**. It consists of a tube of mercury, sealed at one end, with the open end resting in a reservoir also filled with mercury. As the mercury in the reservoir is exposed to variations in the weight of the air, the mercury in the tube rises or drops.

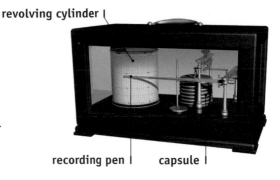

revolving cylinder ⌐

recording pen ⌐    capsule ⌐

⌐ tube

⌐ reservoir

The **aneroid barometer** records variations in atmospheric pressure. Air pressure exerts force on an evacuated capsule. As the capsule contracts or expands, its movement is transmitted to a recording pen, which traces a line on a revolving paper-covered cylinder.

## MEASURING THE WIND

Wind strength and direction are measured with two different instruments. The anemometer, using cups revolving around a mobile axis, transforms the frequency of rotations into a measurable speed. The weather vane indicates wind direction by pointing in the direction it is blowing.

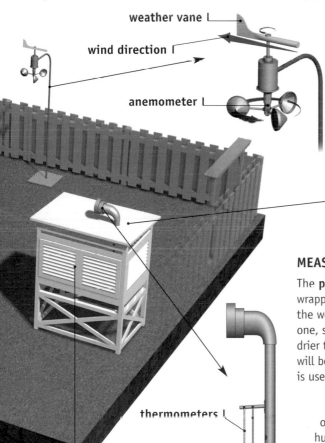

weather vane ⌐

wind direction ⌐

anemometer ⌐

## MEASURING THE TEMPERATURE

Ambient temperature is measured with a **thermometer**. A liquid substance, usually mercury or alcohol, is enclosed in a graduated tube. The liquid expands when the temperature rises and contracts when the temperature drops. Minimum and maximum thermometers record the highest and lowest temperatures in a day.

The **thermometer** is placed in an almost horizontal position.

## MEASURING HUMIDITY

The **psychrometer** uses two thermometers, one wrapped in a wet cloth. As evaporation occurs, the wet thermometer will be lower than the dry one, since evaporation causes cooling. The drier the air, the more the wet thermometer will be cooled. The difference between the two is used to calculate relative humidity.

thermometers ⌐

The reservoir of one ⌐ of the thermometers is wrapped in a **damp cloth**.

To record humidity in the air, older types of **hygrographs** use human hairs, which get longer in humid weather. A stylus attached to a bundle of hairs continuously transcribes variations in humidity onto a roll of paper. Today, electric hygrometers are considered the most accurate.

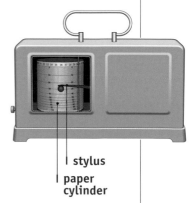

⌐ stylus
⌐ paper cylinder

Meteorologists place some of their instruments in a **Stevenson shelter**, a box that has been painted white and raised 4 feet (1.2 m) above the ground. The sides of the shelter have louvers that allow air circulation and keep solar radiation from directly affecting the instruments.

# Measuring the Temperature

## *Matter in motion*

As strange as it may seem, temperature is simply the measurement of matter in motion. All objects have a temperature, since they are composed of molecules that move more or less quickly. Temperature can be expressed in degrees Celsius (°C), degrees Fahrenheit (°F), or kelvins (K), with no known upper limit. Only the Kelvin scale, however, begins measurement at absolute zero.

### THE THERMOMETER

The thermometer, the instrument used to measure temperature, records the kinetic energy of air molecules when they collide with its glass exterior.

As the air **warms**, its molecules become active and bombard the thermometer. Their kinetic energy is transmitted to the mercury or alcohol contained in the glass tube. As it heats, the liquid expands and rises.

The **colder** the air, the more slowly its molecules move, and the less they collide with the glass of the thermometer. So, the thermometer's liquid stays low.

### CELSIUS AND FAHRENHEIT DEGREES

The Celsius scale (°C), invented in 1742 by the Swedish physicist Anders Celsius, is based on two basic temperatures, those of the freezing and boiling of water (at air pressure of one atmosphere), which were arbitrarily set at 0°C and 100°C. Although the Celsius scale is part of the international system, some countries, including the United States, still use the older Fahrenheit scale, developed by the German physicist Daniel Fahrenheit in 1709. This scale is based on the lowest temperature observed at the time, called 0°F, and an inexact measurement of the temperature of the human body (100°F). According to this scale, water freezes at 32°F and boils at 212°F.

| CONVERSION FORMULAS |
|---|
| °F = (1.8 x °C) + 32 |
| °C = (°F − 32)/1.8 |

**331 K** 136°F (58°C)
El Azizia, Libya:
highest atmospheric
temperature recorded
on Earth

**184 K** -128°F (-89°C)
Vostok, Antarctica:
lowest atmospheric
temperature recorded
on Earth

**273 K** 32°F (0°C)
water freezes

**0 K** -459°F (-273°C)
absolute zero

## ISOTHERMS

The annual average temperature on the surface of Earth is about 59°F (15°C), but there are great differences depending on latitude and time of year. Isotherms are imaginary lines on a map linking places with identical temperatures at a given time. Among other things, isotherms enable us to observe how temperatures change through the seasons.

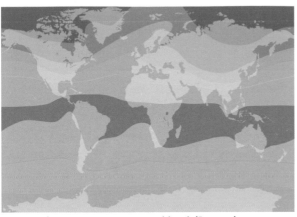

**average air temperatures at ground level (January)**

**average air temperatures at ground level (July)**

| | |
|---|---|
| ■ | > 77°F (> 25°C) |
| ■ | 59°F to 77°F (15°C to 25°C) |
| ■ | 41°F to 59°F (5°C to 15°C) |
| ■ | 14°F to 41°F (-10°C to 5°C) |
| ■ | -22°F to 20°F (-30°C to -10°C) |
| ■ | > -22°F (< -30°C) |

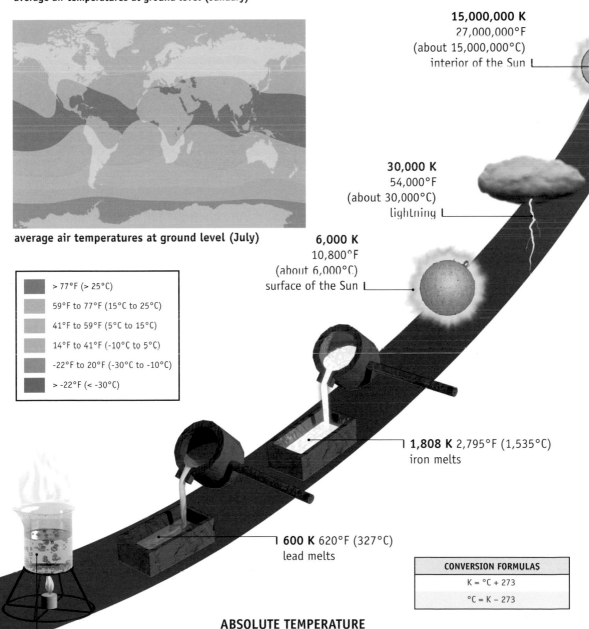

**15,000,000 K**
27,000,000°F
(about 15,000,000°C)
interior of the Sun ⌐

**30,000 K**
54,000°F
(about 30,000°C)
lightning ⌐

**6,000 K**
10,800°F
(about 6,000°C)
surface of the Sun ⌐

⌐ **1,808 K** 2,795°F (1,535°C)
iron melts

⌐ **600 K** 620°F (327°C)
lead melts

| CONVERSION FORMULAS |
|---|
| K = °C + 273 |
| °C = K − 273 |

## ABSOLUTE TEMPERATURE

It is impossible to go below the minimum temperature that scientists call "absolute zero." This value, which equals about −273°C, is the beginning point of the Kelvin (K) scale. A temperature of 0 K corresponds to the unattainable state of matter absolutely devoid of molecular movement.

⌐ **373 K** 212°F (100°C)
water boils

# Balloons and Radar
## *Remote observation of the atmosphere*

Weather stations on Earth take many measurements at ground level, but these readings do not tell us anything about the state of the upper atmosphere. Information on the different air layers and the clouds, which enables us to follow how weather phenomena develop, is acquired through weather balloons and radar.

### THE LIFE AND DEATH OF A WEATHER BALLOON

Inflated with a light gas such as hydrogen or helium, a weather balloon rises ❶ in the atmosphere at an average speed of about 16 feet per second (5 meters per second). As it rises, the radiosonde suspended below the balloon ❷ accumulates measurements and transmits them by radio ❸ to the weather station ❹. When the balloon has reached an altitude of some 19 miles (30 km), the low air pressure at that altitude causes it to burst ❺. A small parachute ❻ deploys to slow the fall of the radiosonde.

Because it is slowed by a **parachute,** the radiosonde hits the ground at only 12 mph (20 km/h), instead of 60 mph (100 km/h), had it been in free fall.

A **superpressure balloon** is covered with a reinforced envelope that enables it to resist variations in atmospheric pressure. When it reaches the upper levels of the stratosphere (22 miles [35 km] altitude), it stops rising. The balloon remains airborne at this altitude for several months, as it is moved by air currents while transmitting data via satellite.

The **reflector** is a paper structure that provides a target for radar.

The **radiosonde**, a tiny automatic weather station, is equipped with sensors that measure the atmospheric pressure, temperature, and humidity. It can also determine its own position, which enables scientists to calculate the wind speed and direction as the balloon rises through the atmosphere.

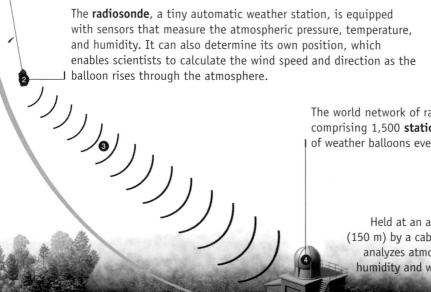

The world network of radiosonde observation, comprising 1,500 **stations,** releases thousands of weather balloons every day.

Held at an altitude of about 490 feet (150 m) by a cable, the **tethered balloon** analyzes atmospheric temperature and humidity and wind speed and direction.

# WEATHER RADAR

By emitting radio waves and measuring the intensity of the radiation that is reflected to it, radar detects the presence, position, and size of objects. The most modern radar instruments are so precise that they can detect masses as small as raindrops.

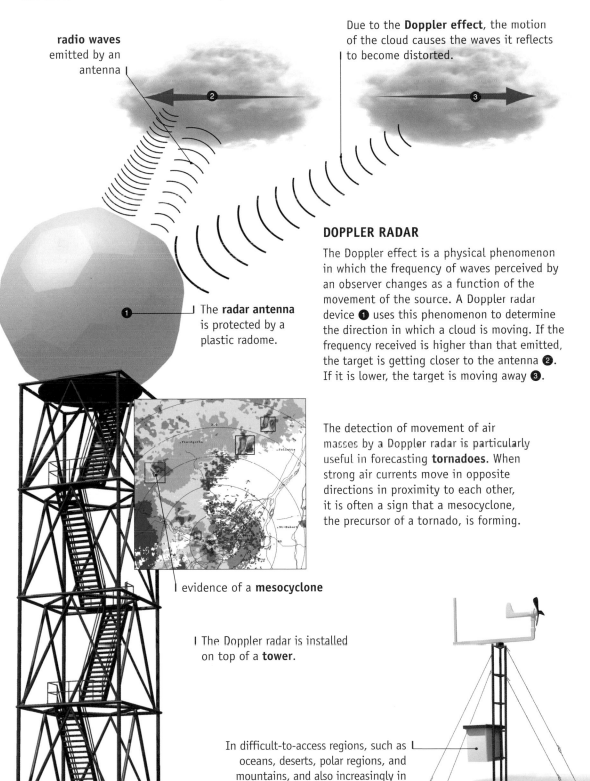

**radio waves** emitted by an antenna

Due to the **Doppler effect**, the motion of the cloud causes the waves it reflects to become distorted.

The **radar antenna** is protected by a plastic radome.

## DOPPLER RADAR

The Doppler effect is a physical phenomenon in which the frequency of waves perceived by an observer changes as a function of the movement of the source. A Doppler radar device ❶ uses this phenomenon to determine the direction in which a cloud is moving. If the frequency received is higher than that emitted, the target is getting closer to the antenna ❷. If it is lower, the target is moving away ❸.

The detection of movement of air masses by a Doppler radar is particularly useful in forecasting **tornadoes**. When strong air currents move in opposite directions in proximity to each other, it is often a sign that a mesocyclone, the precursor of a tornado, is forming.

evidence of a **mesocyclone**

The Doppler radar is installed on top of a **tower**.

In difficult-to-access regions, such as oceans, deserts, polar regions, and mountains, and also increasingly in populated areas, **automatic weather stations** gather data and transmit it by satellite.

# Geostationary Satellites

*Cameras permanently aimed at Earth*

The network of land-based weather stations covers the surface of the continents, but not the oceans. Two-thirds of the planet thus escapes direct observation. Satellites equipped with sensors constantly directed toward the planet, called geostationary satellites, fill this gap and allow meteorologists to follow the development of cloud masses, the formation of hurricanes, and the evolution of ice floes in specific regions.

## IMAGES MADE BY SATELLITES

Using radiometers, satellites record the radiation coming from Earth. Visible radiation can be measured only during daylight, while infrared radiation, which fits between visible light and microwaves, can be observed day and night. The data acquired by the satellites are used to create synthetic images illustrating the distribution of different meteorological phenomena around the planet.

An image created from visible radiation shows the continents and oceans under partial cloud cover ❶. The absence of cloud cover over the Sahara Desert reveals the anticyclonic conditions above it.

In the infrared spectrum, various elements can be perceived depending on the wavelength chosen. Thermal infrared is used to discern variations in temperature. This wavelength also shows differences between high-altitude, or colder, and low-altitude, or warmer, clouds ❷.

Another wavelength in the infrared spectrum shows the distribution of water vapor in the atmosphere ❸.

This composite image, created using different data gathered on June 6, 2000, combines data on ground temperature, temperature on the surface of the oceans, and altitude at the tops of clouds.

## COMPOSITE IMAGES

Meteorological data gathered from different geostationary satellites and ground stations can be digitally combined to form a composite image of Earth. Depending on the need or the effect sought, single parameters, such as ground temperature or the concentration of water vapor, can be shown. Complementary information can be added if desired.

## A SATELLITE BELT

Geostationary satellites orbit over the equator at over 22,000 miles (36,000 km) altitude. Because their movement is synchronized with Earth's rotation, they always cover the same region.

Five geostationary meteorological satellites are distributed around the planet: the U.S. *GOES-West* and *GOES-East*, the European *Météosat*, the Russian *GOMS*, and the Japanese *GMS*. Their observation zones, which partially overlap, cover all of Earth's surface except the polar regions. They are part of World Weather Watch, an international cooperative program set up by the World Meteorological Organization in 1961.

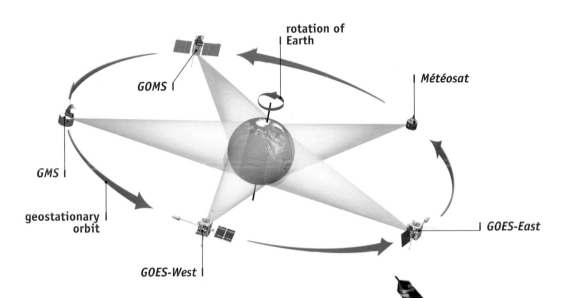

rotation of Earth

*Météosat*

GOMS

GMS

geostationary orbit

GOES-East

GOES-West

## *MÉTÉOSAT,* LONGITUDE 0°

*Météosat,* the European geostationary Earth-observation satellite, is positioned over the Greenwich meridian and covers mainly Africa and Europe. It spins at a speed of 100 rotations per minute as it observes the surface of the planet. Its radiometer gathers atmospheric data on 12 different frequency channels.

The **solar panels** pivot around an axis to follow the apparent movement of the Sun.

The **radiometer** is an instrument used to measure radiation.

**solar panels**

## GOES: ABOVE AMERICA

*GOES-East* and *GOES-West* are the U.S. geostationary environmental-observation satellites, placed at 75° and 135° west latitude, respectively. Each GOES satellite is equipped with two specialized radiometers, a sounder, and an imager.

The **sounder** observes Earth's atmosphere on 19 different channels.

The **imager** is capable of scanning a wide area.

The **magnetometer** measures Earth's magnetic field.

# Orbiting Satellites

Unlike geostationary satellites, whose positions in relation to Earth never change, orbiting satellites constantly circle Earth on a polar orbit. Because of their relatively low altitudes of only between 430 and 930 miles (700 and 1,500 km), they can observe the ground, the oceans, and the atmosphere extremely accurately. The data they gather are regularly transmitted to Earth and used to create weather models and follow changes in the landscape.

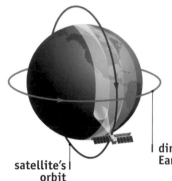

satellite's
orbit

direction of
Earth's rotation

## POLAR ORBIT

Most polar-orbit satellites make fourteen revolutions daily and therefore cover all of Earth's surface. Because of the planet's rotation, the zone they fly over shifts westward with each revolution, but since their orbits are synchronized with the Sun, the same regions are observed at a set time every day.

solar panel

## U.S. MILITARY WEATHER SATELLITES

The DMSP program coordinates a number of weather satellites that gather various types of data used by the Department of Defense of the United States. In 2010, these activities will be merged with the civil NOAA program.

*This nighttime image shows a storm developing in the Mediterranean. Because it was taken in the the light of the full Moon, lit-up cities appear as white spots.*

radiometer

## THE TIROS SATELLITES

American TIROS series weather-observation satellites have been circling Earth since 1970. They are equipped with radiometers that detect visible and infrared radiation, as well as with AMSU microwave detectors that can measure the temperature at different altitudes, even under cloudy conditions.

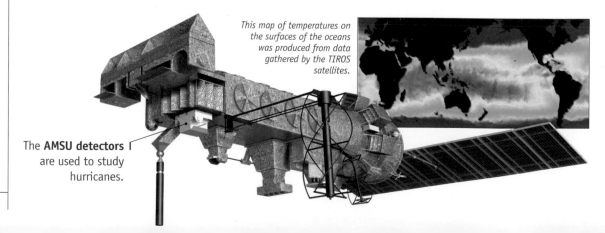

*This map of temperatures on the surfaces of the oceans was produced from data gathered by the TIROS satellites.*

The **AMSU detectors** are used to study hurricanes.

## *TERRA*: WATCHING FOR CLIMATIC CHANGES

The U.S. satellite *Terra*, launched in December 1999, orbits Earth at an altitude of almost 440 miles (705 km). Its five instruments simultaneously measure the properties of clouds, Earth's surface, oceans, vegetation, and particles and gases in the atmosphere and their interactions. These data enable meteorologists to forecast major climatic changes.

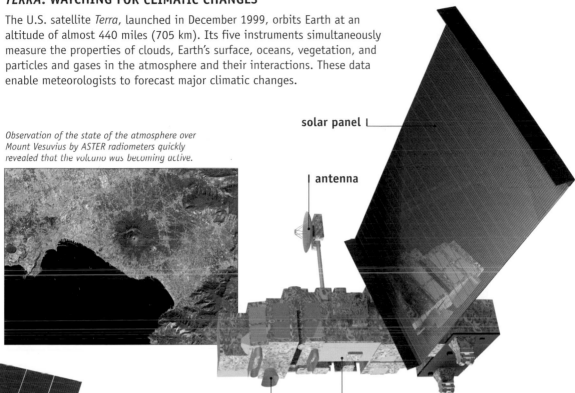

*Observation of the state of the atmosphere over Mount Vesuvius by ASTER radiometers quickly revealed that the volcano was becoming active.*

solar panel

antenna

The **ASTER system** has three very-high-resolution (50 to 295 feet [15 to 90 m]) radiometers.

The nine cameras on the **MISR** radiometer point at Earth from different angles.

## THE EUROPEAN *METOP* SATELLITE

In 2003, European nations will launch their first orbiting weather satellite, called *Metop*, which is part of a joint study program with the United States. Placed at an altitude of about 520 miles (840 km), *Metop* will gather data on the temperature and humidity of the atmosphere, wind speeds, the ozone layer, vegetation, and the polar ice caps.

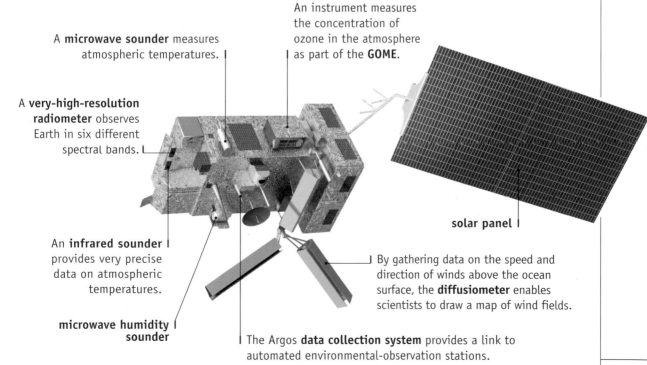

A **microwave sounder** measures atmospheric temperatures.

An instrument measures the concentration of ozone in the atmosphere as part of the **GOME**.

A **very-high-resolution radiometer** observes Earth in six different spectral bands.

solar panel

An **infrared sounder** provides very precise data on atmospheric temperatures.

By gathering data on the speed and direction of winds above the ocean surface, the **diffusiometer** enables scientists to draw a map of wind fields.

**microwave humidity sounder**

The Argos **data collection system** provides a link to automated environmental-observation stations.

# Weather Maps

## *From observation to forecast*

Weather maps are indispensable tools for meteorologists. They provide more information than simple observation of one weather phenomenon because they present an image of a broad geographic area and condense a large amount of information into one place. Millions of measurements taken daily around the planet are used to produce synoptic maps, which illustrate the state of the atmosphere at a specific moment, and forecast maps, which indicate probable changes in atmospheric conditions.

### DATA COLLECTION

At set times several times a day, readings are taken in the network of ground weather stations. On the oceans, information is collected by ships and by automatic stations attached to buoys. Atmospheric conditions are observed at different altitudes by weather balloons, planes, and satellites, while ground-based radar observes the nature and intensity of precipitation. All of this data on humidity, temperature, precipitation, winds, clouds, pressure, and cloud cover is centralized, corrected, and then processed in powerful computers.

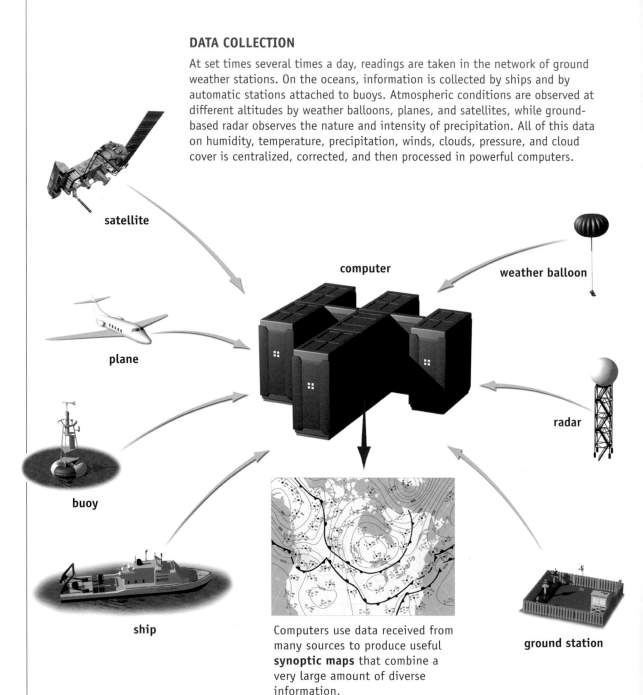

**satellite**

**computer**

**weather balloon**

**plane**

**radar**

**buoy**

**ship**

Computers use data received from many sources to produce useful **synoptic maps** that combine a very large amount of diverse information.

**ground station**

## WEATHER FORECASTING

Forecasting the weather for a particular area is a complex operation involving large quantities of data. Of course, local atmospheric conditions must be taken into account, as must their interactions with conditions in the surrounding regions. Computers are capable of performing several billion calculations per second, and this great processing capacity enables forecasts to be produced very quickly, often just a few minutes after the data are received. Meteorologists sometimes make better forecasts than computers, however, since they can enhance the predictions of the computer's calculations with their knowledge of local factors, such as relief features and watercourses, that influence the weather. The best forecasts,therefore, are made by  human meteorologists using computers.

For the purposes of forecasting calculations, Earth's atmosphere is divided into a **three-dimensional grid** locating millions of points. The future development of weather conditions is calculated for each of these points.

## FORECAST MAPS

Weather forecasts are generally presented to the public with more or less detailed maps that indicate the believed future weather conditions in a region or country, or on an ocean. Some maps, designed, for example, for ships' navigators or airplane pilots, highlight particular features, such as marine weather or air turbulence, respectively. Those made for the public are much more general. No forecast map, however, can guarantee what the weather will be in the future.

**Forecast maps** intended for the general public show only the forecast cloud cover, temperatures, and precipitation. Because of their limited information, they are very easy to read. The graphical symbols used for this type of map are not standardized, but vary according to the organization that produces the map.

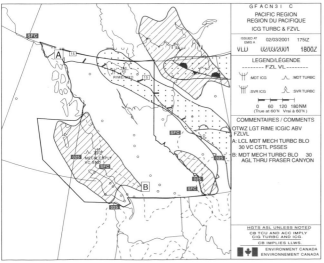

Pilots and airlines use maps showing forecast **turbulence** at high and low altitudes for the areas in which they will be flying. These maps use specific graphical symbols and conventional abbreviations to convey information that is sometimes very complex.

On this map of western Canada, the red hatching indicates forecast zones of turbulence, while planes flying in the regions covered with blue dots may be affected by icing.

# Reading a Weather Map
## *Graphical conventions to describe the weather*

Using a graphical language, a synoptic map presents all of the information gathered by weather-observation stations in a region. Other conventional signs, including isobars, atmospheric fronts, low- and high-pressure zones, and areas of precipitation, are often drawn on the map to make it even more comprehensive.

| FRONTS | |
|---|---|
| ▲▲▲ | cold front |
| ●●● | warm front |
| ▲▲●● | occluded front |
| ▲●▲● | stationary front |

Different kinds of **atmospheric fronts** are symbolized by triangles or semi-circles pointing in the direction in which a particular front is moving.

A low-pressure zone, or **cyclone**, is indicated by the letter L.

A high-pressure zone, or **anticyclone**, is shown by the letter H.

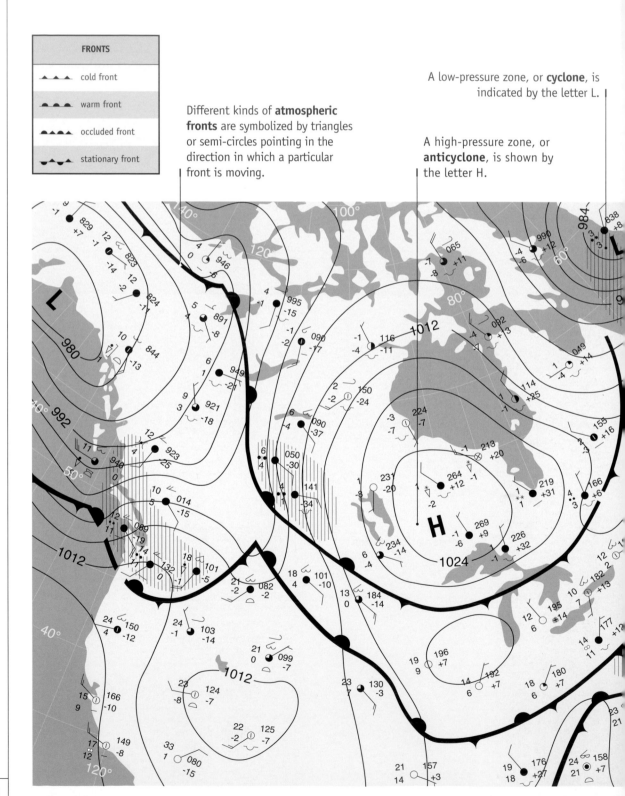

# INTERNATIONAL METEOROLOGICAL SYMBOLS

Each weather station is represented by a circle, around which coded signs express the different measurements of the weather observed. The temperature, cloud cover, types of clouds at different altitudes, precipitation, wind strength and direction, air pressure, and humidity are expressed in a very precise, graphical language that is understood by meteorologists around the globe.

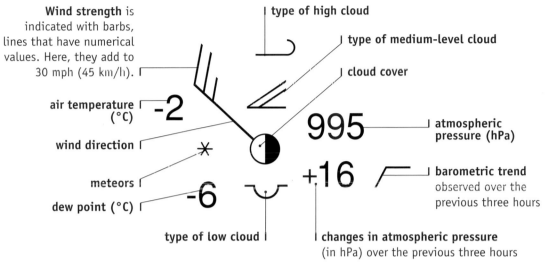

**Wind strength** is indicated with barbs, lines that have numerical values. Here, they add to 30 mph (45 km/h).

air temperature (°C)  -2

wind direction

meteors

dew point (°C)  -6

type of low cloud

type of high cloud

type of medium-level cloud

cloud cover

995  atmospheric pressure (hPa)

+16  **barometric trend** observed over the previous three hours

**changes in atmospheric pressure** (in hPa) over the previous three hours

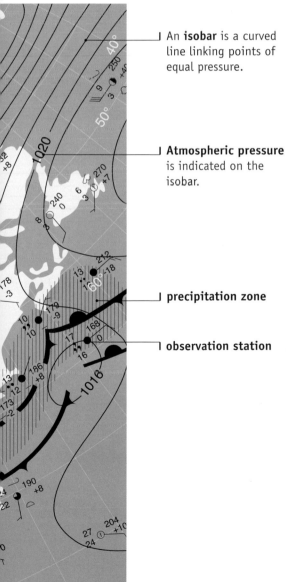

An **isobar** is a curved line linking points of equal pressure.

**Atmospheric pressure** is indicated on the isobar.

precipitation zone

observation station

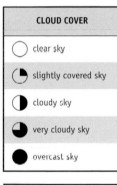

| CLOUD COVER | |
|---|---|
| ◯ | clear sky |
| ◔ | slightly covered sky |
| ◑ | cloudy sky |
| ◕ | very cloudy sky |
| ● | overcast sky |

| WIND STRENGTH | | |
|---|---|---|
| ◯ | still air | |
| / | shaft | 1.25–2.5 mph (2–4 km/h) |
| / | half barb | 5.6 mph (9 km/h) |
| ⊢ | barb | 11.2 mph (18 km/h) |
| ◥ | pennant | 57.2 mph (92 km/h) |

| HIGH CLOUDS | |
|---|---|
| ⌐ | cirrus |
| ꒰ | cirrocumulus |
| 2 | cirrostratus |

| MEDIUM-LEVEL CLOUDS | |
|---|---|
| ⟋ | altostratus |
| ⌣ | altocumulus |

| LOW CLOUDS | |
|---|---|
| — | stratus |
| ⌣ | stratocumulus |
| ⌢ | cumulus |
| ⊿ | cumulonimbus |
| ⟋ | nimbostratus |

| METEORS | |
|---|---|
| 𝟫 | light drizzle |
| 𝟫𝟫 | steady drizzle |
| • | light rain |
| •• | steady rain |
| ✳ | light snow |
| ✳✳ | steady snow |
| ▲ | hail |
| ⌣ | freezing rain |
| ⊿ | ice pellets |
| ≡ | fog |
| ⎿ | storm |
| ⟩⟨ | tornado |
| ♪ | hurricane |

61

# Glossary

**adiabatic:** Due to expansion, occuring without gain or loss of heat.

**centrifugal force:** Inertial force that tends to move away from the center.

**cloud cover:** The amount of cloud above a weather station at a given moment. It is expressed as a fraction of the total area of the sky.

**condensation:** The process by which a gas changes form into a liquid.

**convection:** Ascending movement of a fluid caused by a difference in temperature.

**depletion:** decrease of the amount of a substance.

**DMSP:** Defense Meteorological Satellite Program.

**electric charge:** Quantity of electricity in a substance.

**electromagnetic radiation:** Energy emitted as electromagnetic waves.

**electromagnetic spectrum:** The full range of kinds of electromagnetic radiation.

**evaporation:** The process by which a liquid changes form and becomes a gas.

**GOES:** Geostationary Orbiting Environmental Satellite.

**halo:** A luminous circle that sometimes appears around the Sun or the Moon, caused by the refraction of light by ice crystals in suspension in Earth's atmosphere.

**ice cap:** An area covered with permanent ice, especially in the polar regions.

**infrared:** Having to do with electromagnetic radiation, the wavelength of which is between that of visible light and that of microwaves.

**ionized:** Containing atoms or molecules bearing a positive or negative electric charge, known as ions.

**katabatic:** Moving downward or down a slope.

**kinetic energy:** The kind of energy that all bodies in movement possess.

**latent heat:** Heat absorbed or liberated by a substance when it changes state. As water evaporates, it stores latent heat. When it condenses, water vapor releases this heat into the surrounding atmosphere.

**latitude:** Distance north or south of the equator, measured in degrees.

**microwave:** An electromagnetic wave whose frequency is above 1 GHz.

**orbit:** The curved, usually elliptical path of a satellite around Earth.

**orographic:** Having to do with mountains.

**phenomenon:** An occurrence, fact, or circumstance that is observed or observable.

**pole:** Each of the two points, the North Pole and South Pole, on Earth's surface through which the axis of Earth's rotation passes.

**refraction:** The deviation of the path of a ray as it passes from one medium to another.

**storm:** A type of atmospheric disturbance characterized by violent winds and heavy precipitation; associated with cyclones.

**supercooled:** Remaining liquid at a temperature below the freezing point.

**synchronized:** Moving at the same speed and working exactly together.

**thermopile:** A series of circuits made of two different metals that conduct heat unequally, allowing them to convert temperature into electric power.

**transpiration:** The process by which water passes through a plant, entering through the roots and exiting through the leaves as a vapor.

**tropics:** The terrestrial parallels located at 26°23′ latitude north (Tropic of Cancer) and south (Tropic of Capricorn), corresponding to the places at which the Sun is highest at the solstices.

**turbulence:** Irregular motion of the atmosphere.

**ultraviolet:** Having to do with invisible, electromagnetic radiation, the wavelength of which is between that of light and that of X-rays.

**wavelength:** The distance between two successive crests of a wave.

# Books

The Facts on File Dictionary of Weather and Climate (The Facts on File Science Dictionaries). Jacqueline Smith, editor (Facts on File, Inc.)

Instant Weather Forecasting. Alan Watts (Sheridan House)

The Invention of Clouds: How an Amateur Meteorologist Forged the Language of the Skies. Richard Hamblyn (Farrar Straus & Giroux)

MacMillan Encyclopedia of Weather. Paul Stein (MacMillan Library Reference)

National Audubon Society First Field Guide: Weather (National Audubon First Field Guides). Jonathan D. Kahl (Scholastic Trade)

Nature's Fury: Eyewitness Reports of Natural Disasters. Carol Garbuny Vogel (Scholastic Paperbacks)

Tornadoes (World Life Library). H. Michael Mogil (Voyageur Press)

The Vital Guide to Weather. Brian Cosgrove (Airlife Pub Ltd)

The Weather and Its Secrets. Philip Eden (Readers Digest)

Weather (Factfinder Guide). Ian Westwell (Thunder Bay Press)

Weather (The Golden Guide Series). Paul E. Lehr (St. Martin's Press)

# Videos and CD-ROMs

Extreme Weather (six-volume series). (World Almanac Video)

Understanding: Weather. Discovery Science Understanding series. (Discovery Ch.)

Weather and Climate (CD-ROM). Discovery Channel School Earth Science series. (Discovery Channel)

Weather Extreme. (Discovery Channel)

Weather Predictions. Modern Marvels Science series. (History Channel)

Weather Systems. Understanding Science series. (Dr. Science)

Wild Weather. (Nova)

# Web sites

NSSL's Weather Room
*www.nssl.noaa.gov/edu*

Storms Viewed from Space
*www.athena.ivv.nasa.gov/curric/weather/storm.html*

Visualization of Remote Sensing Data
*rsd.gsfc.nasa.gov/rsd/images/images.html*

WW2010: The Online Guides
*ww2010.atmos.uiuc/(Gh)/guides/home.rxml*

# Index